Charisma
of the Spirit

Charisma of the Spirit

In Search of a Supernatural Experience:
A Journalist Looks at the Tongues Movement

By Rene Noorbergen

PACIFIC PRESS PUBLISHING ASSOCIATION
Mountain View, California
Omaha, Nebraska
Calgary, Alberta

Dedicated to

ELLIE
with love—always
from
Rene—your son

Library of Congress Catalog Card No. 73-91042

Appreciation

Sincere appreciation for advice and counsel provided me while writing this manuscript goes to Dr. Thomas H. Blincoe of Andrews University, Berrien Springs, Michigan; Dr. Douglas Bennett, and Dr. Robert Francis, both of Southern Missionary College, Collegedale, Tennessee.

The counsel and friendship provided by these three scholars will always remain in my mind as true examples of Christian fellowship. Their willingness to serve as advisers in this sensitive subject and their knowledge of the personages of the Godhead have supplied the foundation on which I could build.

Rene Noorbergen

July, 1973
Collegedale, Tennessee

1

Something big is happening in Christianity—something so appealing to so many that it may well alter the shape of the religious world.

The first inkling of it came to me during a visit from two young men to our Washington home as a follow-up of a previous interview on psychic phenomena.

It was the more vocal of the two visitors, the son of a former Southern Senator, who pointedly brought the issue to the surface within moments after their arrival. Super-confident, and attempting to create an impression of sophistication, he charged full-speed ahead into the hottest topic of the century—glossolalia.

"Speaking in tongues is the ultimate evidence that the Holy Spirit has come into a person's life," he asserted finally after an hour-long discussion. Slowly crossing his immaculately manicured fingers under his chin, he watched our faces for the effect of his carefully measured words. Then he continued, "Only when you can exhibit the ability to speak the language of the Holy Spirit can you be sure that His Spirit resides within you."

Jim stopped and cast a knowing glance at his friend Ed. He had made his point, and now all he had to do was await our confirmation, or so he thought. Sliding halfway out of his chair, he relaxed, and swinging his shoeless feet up onto the coffee table, he waited, confidently.

I must admit, his words had impact. While he had been talking about the tongues, my wife and I both found ourselves groping for the right words with which to counter his statements and hurriedly tried to compile a barrage of Bible texts that would stop his unfamiliar advances. However, having never thoroughly studied the subject before, we were momentarily at a loss—more so since he continued his attack by fencing with 1 Corinthians 14, a chapter with which he was well acquainted. For us it presented some real problems in interpretation.

It was hours later when we finally reached a stalemate: Jim shaking his head in utter disbelief over our unprecedented stubbornness; we determined to further study the subject.

What our resistance did to him I will probably never know, but it had at least one noticeable effect; he never came back.

But his friend Ed did, having stayed away from us for a full two weeks. When he finally knocked on our door one night, it was with a troubled face and a desperate cry for help.

"Remember when I left with Jim?" Ed said softly, glancing about with fear-filled eyes. "I had barely got home with Jim when my eyeballs began to swell. It was a strange sensation at first, and when I looked into the bathroom mirror I could see the swelling increase. Within minutes while I was still watching, I could see the whites of my eyes coming up around the irises. My eyes began to protrude. Deep white ridges began to form around the blue. I looked grotesque." And with his eyes nervously probing every corner of our family room, he continued his story—a nightmarish tale of horror and devil possession.

"After we talked with you that night, I knew I didn't want the tongues; but I didn't tell you that evening that all the pictures of Christ I saw in the books and magazines you showed me looked evil to me. I knew I wanted Christ, but the more that decision hardened within me, the more frightening my surroundings became. I began to see demons groping for me—laughing at me. But when my eyeballs began to protrude, I knew then the devil was really after me." He paused and sighed deeply.

"By now Jim had become scared too," Ed continued. "He rushed me to the Georgetown University Hospital where the doctors diagnosed a severe case of glaucoma without apparent cause. I remained there for almost two weeks; but it really wasn't my eyes that bothered me— It was those devils that came at me all hours of the day and night. With threats and screams they tried to win me over to their side and keep me from believing in Christ.

" 'You're ours!' they howled at me menacingly, prodding me with long pointed fingers. 'You're ours, and you're going to stay ours. Don't go back to them. They're evil. They'll confuse you!'

"Frantically I turned from side to side, clawing around, hoping to escape the hordes of devils that reached out for me; but everywhere I looked, they were waiting for me—waiting, watching, grimacing frighteningly. It was then that I realized they weren't just after my eyes. They were after my mind!

"One devil in particular took an unwholesome delight in telling me that I was one of them. I listened, I fought; and when finally he left, I felt I could relax a little, for I knew I had won. But then—suddenly—I was one of them! I was a devil. I was THE devil. However, as soon as I had joined them, I left them again, for I knew instinctively that I wasn't the devil after all—I was Christ! Hovering over my own godly body, I watched myself going from hill to hill, caressing, blessing people wherever I went. Oh, what a relief to be in the arms of God—to be one with God; to *be* God! But it was in the middle of one blessing that I broke out into uncontrollable laughter, for I knew I wasn't Christ after all. I was the devil!"

On and on went his terrifying story of devil possession, but even in the still moments of that evening, his eyes kept darting from wall to wall.

"You know, even now I have fleeting moments of being the devil," he said forlornly, eyeing us with a confused look in his soft blue eyes. "I know I shouldn't really be here talking to you. They're still around me—pulling at me. They want me to become one of them. They really do!"

It was in the wee hours of the morning when we said Good-bye, but not before Ed had agreed to meet with us again to enable us to examine his problems on Biblical grounds. The next two weeks he returned—on time and alone. He joined us for church, took part in the Lord's Supper, and spent the entire evenings with us embarking on a systematic Bible study.

He was intensely interested, and we were surprised when he didn't appear for our fourth meeting. For two weeks we tried to locate his last known Washington address, and when finally we traced his whereabouts, we discovered he had vacated his apartment and had moved in with relatives somewhere in a South Carolina town.

We phoned him there, and although somewhat reluctant, he did agree to talk to us.

"I had to leave Washington because you confused me," he admitted gruffly. "But it's been a good move, for the devils have left me. They don't bother me anymore. I know now that you were wrong. I shouldn't have gone on seeing you after that first meeting. Jim was right all along—"

For a moment I thought he had hung up. All was quiet on the line; only the soft long-distance hum could be heard.

Then I heard his voice again.

It sounded rather triumphant.

"Know those pictures of Christ I talked to you about? The ones I saw on the magazines in your home?" he questioned. "Well, they still look evil to me. Every time I see Christ's face it looks evil to me. Guess my first impression was right—

"Just thought you'd like to know."

And with a gentle click, Ed broke the connection and moved out of my life. We never heard from him again; yet I do hope that someday Ed will renew the connection—but this time directly with God.

If anything ever made a lasting impression on me, this experience surely did. In the course of my years as a journalist covering the world beat, I had witnessed many changes; but most of them had been deviations from the expected development of history and had always been in the political or the scientific area. Not every change was necessarily a welcome one, but it invariably led the way to new experiences.

In the short time that has elapsed since the 1960's, mankind has taken two giant steps forward: one a surge in the field of technology; the other a leap into a new spiritual awakening, igniting the most explosive charge ever to rupture the Christian world. As a result Christ's legacy of peace and love will never be the same again.

At least not if certain vigorous groups have their way.

A few weeks after that first encounter with Jim and Ed we were again faced with a charismatic enthusiast. A neighbor, a concerned lay member of the Episcopal Church had become involved in a drastically new experience. She mentioned it to us during one of her sporadic visits.

"What do *you* think of the charismatic movement?" she queried.

I wasn't startled—just irritated. Why ask me? A few weeks ago it was tongues, and now the entire movement.

What really *is* happening within Christianity that this phenomenon of tongues has managed to gain such a firm footing?

Nothing can compare to a first-hand confrontation when it comes to gathering facts, and it was in late 1972 that I had my first real live meeting with the charismatics.

While I was sauntering down a Memphis street, a strange sound vibrated against my eardrums; unfamiliar and yet melodious.

"Medi alukan— ala— du aru— shamma shamma. Solama sulama sumala tamaku abada da da kumi sala sala mili amatala shamma shamma balu—

"Ama talla manga diekam oh sila sila aboda take shamma shamma—"

I stopped and stared at the stately thirty-odd-pew church that nestled in one of the staid old residential sections of Memphis, Tennessee. In search for hard facts concerning the manifestation of tongues that had begun to seep through the ever-widening cracks in the doctrinal walls of the country's mainline churches, I had been directed to this solemn-looking fortress-like brick building which for years had effectively safeguarded a traditional Calvinistic heritage.

Yet, somehow this was now changing.

The unrelenting December wind howled threateningly about the church's lone spire, and the wet whirly fingers of rain tugged at me with ever-increasing desperation as I climbed my way to the church's main door.

I shivered.

Clutching the brim of my rain-soaked hat with one hand, and attempting with the other to keep my flapping trench coat tightly closed, I felt for footing on the crumbling concrete steps and leaned my wet weight against the aging door.

Within seconds the eerie squeaks of the rusty hinges mingled freely with a strange melodious mumbling, a mournful whimpering of which had eagerly called out to me while I had sloshed past the church's dimly lit windows mere moments before.

Fingers of sound leaked through the darkened hallway. One moment pleading, the next instant macabre or jubilant, a solitary voice, crowned with a shimmering backdrop of subdued cries of unexplainable ecstasy implored, cried with a throbbing chain of sounds that became more insistent and more captivating in the dark as I continued to shuffle carefully across the foot-worn marble slabs that led to the doors of the sanctuary.

Hat under my arm, coat still dripping, I unobtrusively squeezed through the narrow door leading to the sanctuary and joined the stimulated congregation, taking an outside seat on one of the back pews.

Instantaneously I felt surrounded by a storm of ecstatic excitement that hungrily lapped at every believer.

Wide-eyed, and with raptured attention, all participants—young and old alike—listened entranced to the flood of mystifying sounds gushing forth from the mouth of a young man standing on one of the front pews. He had turned around to address the congregation at the same moment as I had stepped inside the door, and across the uneven sea of moving heads and uplifted hands I watched him critically from my vantage point of self-imposed impartiality.

He was a youngster—reckoned by middle-age standards—perhaps twenty-one or twenty-two years of age, but his supernatural performance more than replaced his pronounced immaturity. There he stood, in stark defiance in his inexperience, speaking, talking, uttering sounds that were definitely not from this part of the world. His wet stringy hair framed a face lost in nervous concentration, but the impression he emitted might have appeared noble or even serene if it had not been for an occasional twitch caused by uncontrollable restlessness.

With his slender hands raised skyward as if reaching for God, he talked continuously, praying in sounds that seemed to have no resemblance to any known language.

Tuned into an unknown power, his moving hands gently caressed the air, begging, demanding something from on high; and with each passing moment, my initial impression that a supernatural force had gained complete control of him became stronger.

It was an aging woman who made me shift my attention to another pew. Up until that moment all the excitement had flowed around her, and either by will or by force she had stayed out of the mainstream of the electrifying ecstasy that had invaded the sanctuary.

Now she suddenly jumped up. Since she was seated in the front of the church, all eyes instantly turned to her.

Resolutely grasping hold of her long pleated skirt, she climbed up on the narrow seat of her pew and motioned agitatingly to the now aroused crowd of believers.

"Stop! Hear? Stop! He is praying!" she cried, completely lost in her words, tears running down her withered red cheeks. "He is thanking God for all His blessings." And waving her arms in the air to evoke even more attention, she continued, flushed with ecstasy, "I know his tongue! It is ancient Indian!"

Her task completed, she quickly slipped down and quietly shriveled up again in her pew, mingling once more with the ecstatic believers. It was one of the most unusual meetings I had ever witnessed. In my career as a journalist I had covered a variety of assignments and been exposed to much babbling and many languages, ranging from Albanian to Zulu. But this was different—very different indeed.

Critically and with a clinical eye, I began to scan the exuberant congregation. There weren't many people in attendance that night, perhaps thirty-five or forty. Yet with eyes closed, one could have made only a wild guess at any approximation of its size. The accumulation of jubilant cries, shouts, and praises echoing from all directions at the same time made it like one tumultuous happening reminiscent of Calvin's view of hopeless souls burning in eternal torment.

By this time the supernatural power had turned the religious meeting into a climax of praise. All hands now eagerly reached, grabbing for a share of their kingdom.

With his hands pronouncing blessings left and right, a middle-aged man, evidently the minister, separated himself from a small group of praying individuals and walked to the pulpit.

"Listen my people—" he shouted, his face beaming with a deep-felt excitement. "This is the Lord you're listening to! He's here. This is the Holy Spirit. This is Pentecost all over again! Praise God! Praise the Lord!" He hurried down from the rostrum again to rejoin his praying people, nervously shaking the fingers of his outstretched hands.

A sudden jarring motion at my shoulder made me turn my head.

My neighbor showed me the reason.

Standing up in his full impressive height of five feet two inches, he, too, had felt the spirit and was joining the experience with his own ecstatic tongue.

"Oh si si kalini— idi ma talu uno— ta kala—" His voice faltered, then picked up speed and clarity. "Ini tola tola muni— taka ka takaka—"

I had occupied a seat at the end of one of the back pews, and as though lost in deep thought, I slowly stood up and walked out, head bowed. None noticed.

"I wonder—" I muttered more to myself than to anyone else. "Am I expected to believe that this is what happened at Pentecost?"

Sudden bursts of "hallelujah," and a wild clapping of hands highlighted by exclamations of joy pierced the access doors to the church's sanctuary. In answer to one of the rousing shouts, I turned in the hallway and cast one last curious peek through the dusty spy window in the door.

Somehow I felt that in leaving I had made the right decision.

By now the congregation was separating into several small prayer groups, and echoes of high-spirited prayers were bouncing freely from wall to wall. In every corner tongues speakers and their interpreters were attempting to gain priority for their unique message of the Holy Spirit. Even the cigar-chewing usher in the back row had joined in, shouting with an emotion-choked voice, "I too want the spirit—I too want the spirit—"

Suddenly I heard the frightened cry of a small child.

I turned and walked out.

I'd never welcomed the return of the wet fingers of rain with as much happiness as I did that night.

Things were moving back into the right perspective.

Because of my professionally motivated studies in the world of psychic phenomena and the supernatural, I had become confronted with questions associated with a manifestation called the "gift of tongues." Its believers and practitioners maintain that through the mysterious workings of the Holy Spirit they have received the same gift of tongues—the power to speak "other" tongues and languages—as was granted to the disciples at Pentecost, when tongues of fire descended upon them signifying that they were filled with the Holy Spirit. It was this promised baptism with God's special power and the resulting ability to speak intelligent foreign languages that made it possible for them to carry out Christ's command to preach the gospel into all the world, reaching non-believers in surrounding nations in their own tongues.

For many years known as a pivotal doctrine of the Pentecostal Church, the ability to speak "other tongues," or as it is often called "unknown tongues," has infiltrated the quiet sanctity and breached the self-imposed doctrinal walls of the mainline Christian churches since the early 1960's under the melodious sounding name of the "charismatic (also known as neo-Pentecostal) movement." It was Dennis J. Bennett, pastor of the sophisticated St. Mark's Episcopal Church in Van Nuys, California, who changed the historical direction of the tongues movement. For several months he had fought a deep emotional struggle affecting his personal spiritual life, and on Sunday morning April 3, 1960, he faced his expectant congregation, looking tense and tired. Some of his parishioners who remember that day say that it gave them a foreboding of a dire announcement.

He did not disappoint them.

Addressing his audience with the utmost sincerity, he confessed reluctantly that he had received the "baptism of the Holy Spirit" in October of the previous year and subsequently had received the ability to speak in tongues.

Reporting on this, *The Nation*, September 28, 1963, quoted him as saying, "The Holy Spirit did take my lips and tongue and form a powerful language and praise and power that I myself could not understand." In the resulting physical and spiritual chaos that engulfed the sanctuary, one of the associate priests removed his ecclesiastical robe, resigned amid great pandemonium, and angrily stamped out of the church.

The end result of Father Bennett's shocking announcement was the submission of his resignation to the 2,500-member church. Later on in the following year he transferred to St. Luke's Episcopal Church in Seattle, where today he is regarded as one of the foremost spokesmen for the charismatic movement and a frequent main speaker at national and international charismatic meetings. In the years that have transpired since that dramatically staged confession, many of the world's leading theologians and ranking historians have begun to rate the influence of the tongues in present-day Christianity on equal par with the Protestant Reformation, for in these short years its impact on the Christian world has been of such magnitude that it can never again be forgotten.

The two leading components of the charismatic movement—speaking in tongues and faith healing—are responsible for its popularity; and even such major secular publications as *Time* and *Life* have recognized the relentless force of these two elements.

Said *Time*, "It is the fastest growing church in the

Hemisphere."—*Time*, Nov. 2, 1962, p. 56. *Life* called it "the Third Force—a development as important as was the birth of Catholicism and Protestantism."—"The Third Force in Christendom," *Life*, June 9, 1958, p. 113. Still others have prophetically labeled it the "New Revival Movement," the "Wielding Ax of God," the "New Penetration," or simply "The Return of God's Own Church."

Statistics are often a poor way of proving a point, as their meaning tends to vary with each biased interpreter. Yet they are indicative when studying the growth of a movement.

Recent figures (1972/73) reveal that the charismatic movement has quietly invaded over 50 distinctly different Protestant denominations, and no less than 2,500 clergymen of churches affiliated with the National Council of Churches now practice the "gift of tongues" with or without the spiritual participation of their congregations. In fact, in many cases the parishioners or congregations have no knowledge of these activities of their spiritual shepherds. Once ultraconservative, the Methodist Church harbors within its fold tongues-speaking lay members and clergymen. The Episcopalians, too, have embraced its principles so strongly that their leaders and those of the Assemblies of God (one of the original Pentecostal groups) have seen the need to meet in conferences to discuss their mutual problems associated with the growing "ministry of the Holy Spirit."

The Baptists speak in tongues. The Southern Baptist Convention, the American Baptist Convention, and the Baptist Bible Fellowship display within their ranks leading theologians who unashamedly practice their new-found spiritual gifts. The Presbyterian Church also is affected, while almost 10 percent of all Lutheran congregations in the United States boast of active glossolalia cells in their midst. Even the once so staunch and conservative Dutch Reformed and Christian Dutch Reformed Churches have been infiltrated with remarkable success.

Exact figures concerning this movement are always difficult to obtain, and most of those available are quite often short of complete accuracy, as all are based on "reliable estimates."

Opinions as to the number of Catholics who practice the Pentecostal phenomena around the world vary greatly. Most recent figures dealing with the interest in the United States alone show that up to 300,000 Roman Catholics are convincingly involved. Worldwide Catholic involvement may approximate 20 million. The Directory of Charismatic Prayer Groups listed 350 active groups in the United States and abroad in 1971, a figure which soared sharply to 625 just a year later. In 1973 this number had grown to 1,250. A similar growth was evident at the International Conference on Charismatic Revival. These meetings, held at Notre Dame University, had an attendance of 1,250 in 1970; 5,500 in 1971; 11,500 in 1972 and 20,000 in 1973, and in a recent interview with Auxilliary Bishop Joseph McKinney of Grand Rapids, Michigan, the leading figure in the Catholic charismatic movement, I was informed that there is no indication that this rate of growth is on the decline. "It is certainly one of the most significant developments in the church today, and most of my colleagues look approvingly on these Pentecostals," he told me unreservedly.

The question as to whether his "baptism of the Holy Spirit" as mentioned in various national publications really meant that he also has the ability to speak in tongues remained unanswered until our interview. His reaction was honest and straightforward when I asked him about it.

"I have always told people I haven't," he replied. "But recently a couple of times I think that I have had a kind of induced form that I really hesitated to do. But somehow or other, being with the people and noticing their freedom, I have suddenly become conscious of the fact that I have restricted myself in places where I shouldn't because of my background and orientation. So for this reason once in a while I do that when others are doing it just to permit myself to say—to utter syllables that are not words, this with the intention and the resolve and the attempt to open myself up and praise God in the best way I can, because this is what real tongues are." This statement, coming from the man who was recently appointed by the nation's bishops to oversee the movement, is significant.

Time magazine says this about "The Pentecostal Tide":

"Catholic Pentecostalism is notably less emotional than the classical Protestant form," says one observer. "There is less reliance on the literal interpretation of biblical prophecies, less emphasis on the imminence of a Second Coming. Catholic Pentecostals also insist that they are completely loyal to the church, but they consider a continuing renewal essential."

"The movement," the *Time* report continues, "won powerful new support at the Notre Dame conference [in 1973]. It came from Leo-Jozef Cardinal Suenens, the

Primate of Belgium and one of the most progressive voices in the church's hierarchy. It was his personal intervention on the floor of Vatican II that helped sway council opinion to the view that the gifts of the Holy Spirit are not exclusively experiences of ancient Christianity but a continuing force in the modern church as well. Suenens was greatly impressed by the fervor of the Pentecostal phenomenon during a tour of the U.S. last year, and returned this spring for a visit to U.S. Charismatic centers. Though he is still a staunch champion of 'co-responsibility' of the bishops with the Pope, Suenens now emphasized that structural reforms must be accompanied by spiritual renewal. 'The gifts of the spirit are given especially to build up the Christian community,' he told the stadium crowd at Notre Dame. 'After Vatican II we had to make a series of reforms, and we must continue to do so. But it is not enough to change the body. We need to change the soul to renew the church and the face of the earth.'

"Is Suenens himself a Charismatic? He has said that he is 'personally involved' in the movement, but when *Time* asked him specifically whether he had received the Holy Spirit baptism at a charismatic prayer meeting, he declined to answer, saying that his private spiritual life was 'too delicate.'

"Still, the cardinal's support was unequivocal. He conceded that there could be excess among the Pentecostals, noting that 'when you light a lamp in the darkness, you will draw some mosquitoes.' But he praised the leaders for their 'sound theology, common sense and wisdom.' Indeed, he said, the Pentecostal renewal is 'not a movement. It is a current of grace . . .

growing fast everywhere in the world. I feel it coming, and I see it coming.' And to the stadium crowd: 'You are in such a special way the people of God.' "—*Time,* June 18, 1973, p. 91.*

That the tongues speakers are not merely limited to the continental United States is attested to by theologians and researchers from both Latin America and Europe. Alan Walker, who discussed the explosive situation with many leaders on both of these continents, relates this in his book, *Breakthrough—Rediscovery of the Holy Spirit* (Nashville, Tenn.: Abingdon Press, 1964).

"The Pentecostal Church in South America has become the fastest growing church in the world," he relates on page 10. "In Chile since 1930, Pentecostalism has doubled itself every ten years. On the continent as a whole, there could be five or six million people linked to the movement." This was true in 1964, and if the rate of growth has continued on the aforementioned scale, which is a realistic possibility, then by 1973 the number might well have mushroomed to ten million.

In neighboring Brazil, a dramatic change in religious emphasis has also been experienced as a direct result of the work of the charismatics. Whereas in 1930, only 9.5 percent of the Protestant segment of the population admitted belief in Pentecostalism, by 1964, according to Waldo A. Cesar, they comprised 73.6 percent of all Protestants. These facts come from Waldo A. Cesar's book, *Protestantismo e Imperialismo na America Latina* (Rio de Janeiro: Vozes, 1968), page 105.

And Europe? It is no different there, as a recent

---

*Reprinted by permission from TIME, The Weekly Newsmagazine; Copyright Time Inc.

fact-finding tour indicated. It has also become a spiritual boiling pot, and no single group will admit this as readily as the Europeans!

While traveling in Europe in late 1972, I spent several days in the Netherlands and had numerous encounters with the Navigators, members of the Youth for Christ movement and the Campus Crusade. With its 13 million inhabitants quite equally divided between the Catholic Church and a conglomeration of Protestant denominations (not to mention the large number of political parties closely aligned with these churches), this age-old bastion of liberty and free speech has for many years been overripe for a change. This change, it appears now, is in the making.

What is happening in this industrious little country behind the dikes is tremendous. Christ-centered coffee bars scattered throughout the country attract hundreds of youth every night. Dutch Reformed pastors beg Youth for Christ leaders to "take over" in their neighborhoods, admitting that their churches are dying if not already dead! One television commentator smilingly told me of the American ambassador and his wife and their widely reported conversion to Christ. The Bible study group, meeting in their private quarters, was recently featured on Dutch National television.

Voice, the organ of the Full Gospel Business Men's Fellowship International (FGBMFI), gives this report on progress in the Netherlands:

"At a summer Bible Conference camp in Holland, had we been able to remain another day we would have had the privilege of teaching in a tent that seats 3,000. They invited us to return next year for an entire week.

"In two cities, Eindhoven and Almelo, the churches were so packed they set chairs in the aisles. . . . The leader, who was a physics professor at the university, said that the Spirit breathed afresh, and we continued to pray with the people for deliverance and healing until almost eleven o'clock."—*Voice*, November, 1972, p. 22.

Everywhere I went I heard of the revolutionary change that is supposedly taking place. Old barges, abandoned windmills, World War II airplane hangars, and even out-of-the-way stables are used by the zealous converts in their attempts to organize new meeting places and form new groups. The Jesus People, many of whom share spiritual aims almost identical with those of the American charismatics, have vowed that they will introduce the Holy Spirit to every major population center in the Benelux countries (Belgium, Netherlands, Luxembourg); and judging from their actions and reactions, they are well on their way. Are their leaders perhaps too young and too inexperienced to lead whole nations to Christ?

Christianity Today asked the same question on its European investigative mission. The answer it reported typifies the European charismatics. "Jesus is in a hurry to reach the world," voiced one of their leaders; "therefore we must be in a hurry too."—*Christianity Today*, Oct. 13, 1972, p. 24.

Everywhere I traveled—Germany, England, Belgium, France, Sweden, Denmark, Norway, and Finland—I met with the same reaction.

"Jesus People, you say? Charismatics? Tongues? They're all over! They're completely upsetting our formal religious life," one Swedish clergyman reacted.

"We'd just as well pack up and go home. They're beginning to take over our churches." Nightclub dates for musical presentations telling about their supernatural experiences are common occurrences to Scandinavian charismatics. Jesus concerts, Jesus Day festivals, door-to-door witnessing campaigns, and organized attempts to reach the socially downtrodden as well as the upper strata of society are the order of the day.

Raymond W. Becker, editor of *Voice*, reported the following about a recent Full Gospel effort in Finland:

"In Turku, the last Finnish city we were in, over 35 young people received the baptism. The Lord spoke forth in prophecy, saying He was going to use them . . . that He was melting and molding Finland and its people . . . that now the fullness of the harvest is coming and that He will thrust them out into all parts of the world . . . that what God has hereunto done in that country is only a whisper . . . and that these young people will be a mighty shout to the European countries and even their enemies will kneel and praise the Lord with them."—*Voice*, October, 1972, p. 14.

Christianity Today points out how far the Scandinavian youth have already progressed in their endeavor to capture souls for Christ. "YWAM [Youth With a Mission] also sponsors a center at Christiana, a run-down former army base in Copenhagen that is one of the worst hell holes on earth," it says, relating to the activities of one of the groups. "More than 1,000 hippies, junkies, pushers, sex freaks, witches, Satan worshippers, and mental cases from all over the world live there in assorted communal arrangements—amid disease and absence of the law. There are overdose deaths nearly every month. . . . Despite the depravity some have come to Christ. 'God is scooping up the scum of the earth and making something beautiful out of it,' reflected a repentant alumnus of Christiana."—*Christianity Today, op. cit.*

As on the Continent, the same thing is happening in the British Isles and also in Communist Eastern Europe. Even the traditional Gypsies in Southern Europe are now engaged in the movement, for it has been estimated that at least 25,000 of them are presently evangelizing all over the Riviera and the Costa Brava with their strange new tongues, thereby transforming not only their traditional image but their *modus operandi* as well.

All these groups may be operating under different names, but their goals are the same. They want to reach people for Christ before it is too late. It's only love they're after—to receive and to spread, they say. "We need the Spirit's manifestations now!" one young crusader pointed out to me. "Once that happens, everything else will fall into place!"

Although there are undeniable similarities between the Pentecostals and the charismatics, the latter have seemingly divorced themselves from any official connection with their founding fathers. No study of the charismatic movement, however, can be considered complete without examining the modern foundation supporting the tongues-speaking movements.

It all began around the turn of the century when Charles F. Parham, a young Methodist minister, dissatisfied with his personal spiritual condition, became determined to do something about it. Reasoning that only a true rebirth and a rediscovery of the "gifts of the

spirit" would bring him into absolute harmony with
God, he set out to establish a Bible school in an
abandoned mansion in Topeka, Kansas, to be utilized as
a "spiritual discovery center."

The building chosen for the school was sarcastically
known as Stone's Folly, so named because the builder
ran out of money halfway through its construction. This
stigma, however, did not in any way hamper Parham's
zeal. With forty students he initiated a study into the
gifts and fruits of the Holy Spirit, hoping to discover
whether there was possibly one specific element common to all of those who in Biblical times had received
the outpouring of the Holy Spirit.

It was not until December of that year (1900) that a
substantial consolidated effort emerged. Parham was
scheduled to embark on a three-day trip and decided
that in the interim his students should undertake an
intense study of the book of Acts.

"Study every account in Acts where the baptism of
the Spirit was received," he charged them, "and find out
whether there was a common denominator."

Returning three days later, he found his school
buzzing with excitement, for "on five occasions where
the Holy Ghost was received," he was told, "it was
followed by the phenomena of speaking in tongues.
Could this perhaps be what we're looking for?"

A methodical comparison of the texts showed that in
certain instances there had indeed been a connection
between the Holy Spirit and tongues, and in order to
test its validity in modern times, a marathon prayer
session was decided upon. Beginning at daybreak the
following morning, prayers for the outpouring of the

Holy Spirit were sent up in vain repetition. The morning passed, and so did the afternoon—yet the Spirit did not come. It was not until early that evening at approximately seven o'clock that one of the students, Agnes N. Ozman, remembered something important.

John L. Sherril describes what developed. Here is his account:

"Wasn't it true that many of the baptisms described in Acts were accompanied by an action, as well as prayer? Didn't the person offering the prayer often put his hands on the one who wished to receive the baptism? In the Bible she found the reference she remembered. There it was: at Samaria, at Damascus, at Ephesus, always the word 'hands.' 'Putting his hands on him—' 'Then laid they their hands on them—'

"Miss Ozman went to find Charles Parham. She told him about her new thought.

" 'Would you pray for me this way?' she asked.

"Parham hesitated just long enough to utter a short prayer about the rightness of what they were doing. Then, gently he placed his two hands on Miss Ozman's head. Immediately, quietly, there came from her lips a flow of syllables which neither of them could understand.

"The Pentecostals look back on this hour—7:00 p.m., New Year's Eve, 1900, as one of the key dates in their history. They point to it as the first time since the days of the early church that the baptism of the Holy Spirit had been sought, where speaking in tongues was expected as the initial evidence."—*They Speak With Other Tongues* (A Spire Book), page 38.

Once the discovery of the common denominator had

been established, the news spread rapidly throughout America. Fighting fierce opposition from both clergy and lay members, Parham took to the street corners to propagate his teachings. When subsequently informed that Stone's Folly would be sold from under him, he moved his operations to Houston, Texas, and continued his work from there.

By this time his efforts had begun to receive serious recognition, for his preaching was dynamic. He proclaimed that only the "full gospel" could save; that is, the gospel in its entirety, complete with tongues, faith healing, and other gifts as promised to accompany the reception of the Holy Spirit. Consequently, faith healing was soon added to the list of Pentecostal manifestations.

One of Parham's Houston students, W. J. Seymour, exported the full gospel to the West Coast, fertile ground for many a religious sect, linking his name permanently to 312 Azusa Street, Los Angeles—an address that was to become a Pentecostal mecca for years to come.

An ordained Negro minister, Seymour had arrived in Los Angeles to take over the congregation of a small segregated church, but as soon as he opened his series of sermons and announced his intention to preach on the Holy Spirit and speaking in tongues, the church elders, having previously heard of the religious aberration, as they regarded it, protested vehemently. When Seymour returned for his second sermon, he found the church doors barred. His congregation had formally rejected him.

Accepting the invitation of a dissenting church member, Seymour soon found himself presenting the remainder of the series in her home. For three days he preached there, expounding on the teachings of the Holy Spirit. On the evening of the third day it happened. As he was talking, his listeners suddenly broke out in a rash of tongues, speaking, laughing, and singing, using syllables they never knew existed. It caused such wild enthusiasm that when the spontaneous shouts of Hallelujah and ceaseless clapping had reached a deafening crescendo, the roof caved in, and the rafters crashed down. This signaled the end of the meeting.

Having now proved the validity of his claims in the eyes of his followers, Seymour had no trouble at all finding a suitable meeting place. This time it was an old abandoned livery stable on Azusa Street, wedged in between a stable and a tombstone factory.

Some who witnessed the scenes that took place there for the next 1,000 days called it a true spiritual revival. With often more praying than preaching, Seymour led out but allowed others to take over whenever possible. His believers came from everywhere—New England, Canada, Great Britain—and no one was sent away. There is little doubt in the minds of the old-time Pentecostals when asked to identify the place where their full-gospel movement received its greatest single thrust.

"It was in Stone's Folly that the movement was born," they rightly claim. "But it would have died a quiet and painless death if it had not been for the Azusa Street Mission."

Much has changed since the early days of Pentecostalism. The early movement was marked by the low educational level of its converts. It generally consisted of those who did not feel at home in main-line churches, partly because of the class distinction found there.

Carroll Stegal, a conscientious student of Pentecostalism, wrote:

"The appeal of Pentecostalism is limited quite clearly to the naïve and gullible mind which will accept things without investigation. The great majority of the followers of the healers are old people, shallow people— people cast aside by society and forgotten by the proud 'established churches,' to our eternal discredit."—Carroll Stegal, Jr., *The Modern Tongues and Healing Movement.*

Not only were class barriers absent in the Pentecostal circles; racial barriers were also missing. Today the social and organizational structure of the early pioneer Pentecostal churches has changed. The semi-educated and unskilled are still welcome and, in fact, still comprise a high percentage of the old-time Pentecostal church. But a new breed, the intellectuals, have taken control of its once loosely knit congregations. Their full gospel emphasis, however, has remained intact.

While there is no basic difference between the old-time Pentecostals and the charismatics or neo-Pentecostalists, the latter prefer to be classified under one of those new names as it distinguishes them from a movement which was once considered to consist of only the ignorant and emotionally unstable. As a rule, the charismatics try to involve themselves in the phenomena of speaking in tongues and spiritual healing practices without entering into ecstatic behavior so characteristic of some of the Pentecostal churches. Another difference is in the social makeup of most of their groups. In marked contrast to their heritage-builders, the charismatic groups appeal predominately to the educated, and this thrust, together with their rather sophisticated use of tongues, has gained them thousands of converts in the upper strata of society. Today doctors, lawyers, educators, and businessmen find that they can combine their basic desire for a "new birth" with a tongues experience—without becoming the topic of ridicule from their friends and neighbors.

Mrs. Jeane Stone, board member of the Blessed Trinity Society, a group formed by Harold Bredesen, a Dutch Reformed minister and avid tongue enthusiast, says of these tongues:

"Their private use is more important than public, more oriented to clergy and professional classes, more Bible-centered as against experience, not separatist, more orderly meetings with strict adherence to Pauline directives, less emphasis on tongues."—As quoted by Frank Farrell, "Outburst of Tongues: The New Penetration," in *Christianity Today*, September 13, 1963, p. 6.

The question as to whether the charismatic movement is strictly a spontaneous outlet for emotional ecstasy, leading to a sense of spiritual fulfillment, can be answered in the negative. There are undoubtedly those who feel themselves attracted to the movement and join on their own initiative, but the majority of converts are sought out through a conscientious missionary endeavor —often by individual converts but more often by organizations such as the Full Gospel Business Men's Fellowship International, a California-based religious enterprise led by its founder Demos Shakarian. A wealthy businessman, he formed his organization after having been encouraged in the idea by the spiritual activist Oral Roberts.

In typical newspaper style, the New York *Times*

carried the following report on the organization in a dispatch dated July 16, 1972.

"A businessmen's group closely associated with the Pentecostal movement, which gives special attention to the phenomenon of 'speaking in tongues,' reported this week that its membership had doubled in the last two years.

"The Full Gospel Business Men's Fellowship International, whose headquarters are here [Los Angeles], made the membership report after its 19th world convention in San Francisco. Leaders of the 21-year-old fellowship attributed the growth in large part to increased interest in the Pentecostal movement among Roman Catholics.

"The gift of tongues, or glossolalia, is the power of speaking in a polyglot congregation so that everyone hears his own tongue. The phenomenon was experienced by some in the early days of the Christian church, but the Pentecostal movement in the United States is generally traced to the first decade of the century.

"Until the last 10 years, the controversial phenomenon of speaking in languages never learned by the speaker, nor understood by the hearer, has usually been associated with holiness or Pentecostal church groups, the largest of which is the Assemblies of God.

"However, the Full Gospel Business Men's Fellowship is part of a recent fluid movement that includes both 'old-time' Pentecostals and 'mainline' church members who join outpourings of prayer and praise.

"Demos Shakarian, 58 years old, founder and president of the fellowship, told more than 6,000 delegates to the San Francisco convention that by the beginning of next year, the fellowship would reach as many people as it did during its first 20 years.

" 'God is using the fellowship to bring the Holy Spirit movement and His gifts back to the people,' said Mr. Shakarian, a dairy farmer and shopping center developer of Armenian descent who lives here.

"The fellowship now has an estimated total of 300,000 adherents in 900 chapters throughout the world. Some 700 are in the United States and Canada."

The Shakarian family is no newcomer to the Pentecostal experience. They proudly point out that one of the first Pentecostal churches in North America was established in their California home as a direct result of their interest in the Azusa Street Mission. Their experience, however, with the supernatural was evident long before this, for *The Shakarian Story*, by Thomas Nickel, (FGBMFI, 1964), reveals that the family has been involved in direct revelation, vision, speaking in tongues, and miraculous healings for over 100 years, predating their arrival in America by many years.

Dissatisfied with the spiritual condition of humanity in general, the FGBMFI has taken it upon itself to implant within the narrow boundaries of the traditional churches the manifestations of Pentecostalism; and in order to accomplish this, the organization sponsors banquets, conventions, breakfasts and informal gatherings throughout the world on a local, national, and international level. Being astute businessmen and full-gospel Pentecostalists, the Shakarians do not leave a stone unturned to attain their goal.

Says Russel T. Hitt: "The most polished of public relations techniques have been enrolled to advance the movement. While there is certainly nothing wrong with using modern techniques, the Neo-Pentecostalists cannot claim complete spontaneity."—"The New Pentecostalism: An Appraisal," in *Eternity*, July, 1963, p. 16.

Because members of the FGBMFI are firm believers in miracles, supernatural phenomena, and faith-healing, much of what the organization does is based on the feeling that all their efforts are backed by godly power. Nothing stands in their way because of revelations they attribute to God.

One of these "revelations" occurred at the opening service of a series of meetings held in early July, 1972, when Rex Humbard addressed 4,000 FGBMFI believers. Speaking "in prophecy," one of the members addressed the group in the following words:

"These days are anointed of God, saith the Holy Ghost. You shall treat them as holy days and as days of reverence, for before these meetings are finished I will reveal Myself to you in My Word. I shall reveal Myself to you in a greater and more immeasurable way. I will show you not only things to come, but the great things of the here and now. In these days you shall understand Me more as your Saviour, and as your Baptizer in the Spirit. In these days you shall understand Me in a greater way as the Miracle Worker. You shall know more of Me as your Healer, and in these days you shall come to know Me in a supernatural and a new way as the great Resurrection."

With unmatched zeal they spread their full-gospel message, using among other things, their monthly publication, *Voice*, which enthusiastically publicizes such happenings and testimonies as "baptisms in the spirit" and other related topics.

Carefully they select new targets for their full-gospel emphasis. In January, 1973, a new thrust was added to those already in progress. Regarding the Seventh-day Adventist Church as spiritually impoverished because it does not endorse their "gift of tongues," they decided to "enrich" it. They began mailing a copy of their monthly *Voice* to influential Adventist leaders around the country hoping to repeat the impact a similar effort had earlier on another major denomination in the United States.

2

Several times in this past year I have patiently listened to glossolalists who have pointed out to me that anyone who lacks the gift of tongues simply cannot be filled with the Holy Spirit. I'm not so sure. Throughout recorded history there have been many occasions where religious zealots have been observed speaking in ecstatic tongues; in fact, almost all the known accounts of tongues speaking predating the Pentecostal experience are of pagan origin; and as these pagan religions were based on satanic-oriented cults, those early pre-Pentecost ecstatic tongues experiences were doubtless of satanic origin.

Presuming this will not or cannot happen again is like

saying that Satan does not have the power to repeat his deceptions. But Satan *does* exist, and the Bible tells us that he will continue his attempts to deceive the minds of men until God calls on him for a final accounting.

Pat Boone, for one, is not at all ready to accept the view that the devil repeats himself. In his book, *A New Song*, he describes his initiation into the experience of speaking in tongues. Pat relates that while he was lying in bed one night he suddenly became aware that his wife was whispering something to herself.

" 'What, honey,' I asked; 'what are you saying?'

"In her drowsy state, she hadn't realized that she'd been mumbling audibly. 'I don't know what I am saying,' she replied. 'It's just a phrase from my prayer language. I've heard myself saying it over and over.'

"I listened closely, because naturally I was intrigued. I wasn't expected to understand what she was saying, but suddenly I was transfixed. My wife was praising the Lord—in Latin! I knew she had never had a day of Latin, but I had studied it four years. Yet now she was saying very distinctly, 'Ave Deum! Ave Deum! Ave Deum!' or 'Praise God,' in a language she'd never learned.

"When I told her, she began to weep and immediately knelt by the bed and began truly to praise her Lord in a lovely flow of the most beautiful language I've ever heard. In awe, and gratitude, I knelt beside her and thanked God for confirming to both of us, in a way only He could have devised, that this language was truly a gift of His Spirit. Would, or could, Satan have caused Shirley to 'praise God' in words she'd never learned and didn't even understand, except in her spirit? Inconceivable!"—Pat Boone, *A New Song* (Carol

Stream, Illinois: Creation House), pages 117, 118.

If the utterings themselves are to be the criteria of their genuineness, then every lie of Satan should be accepted as truth. The phenomenon of glossolalia cannot merely be accepted at face value. Too much depends on a correct understanding.

The evidence of historical incidents of glossolalia (ecstatic tongues) (derived from *lalein glōssais* [Greek] meaning "speaking in tongues") in paganism are too numerous to ignore. There is no Biblical or scientific foundation whatsoever for the position that every vocal utterance—no matter how strange or weird—has to be an expression of the will of God or has to be the voice of God; yet many who practice ecstatic speech subscribe to this view.

When, as a journalist, I research a story and probe into the background of a reported event endeavoring to establish precedents, I don't stop searching and checking when I stumble upon a report that tends to prove a preconceived point. Researching means digging for facts, no matter where the trail of evidence may lead; and only when I have gathered the available facts do I begin examining, comparing, and evaluating the accumulated material. Then only can true conclusions be reached.

Knowing how sincere many of the neo-Pentecostalists are, I would like to see them backtrack on the trail of historical evidence and try to establish a factual foundation for themselves, without having to lean on the opinion of those with preconceived ideas. Can they prove that what they're experiencing today is indeed the equivalent of an original godly gift? Somehow it seems too convenient to look at Pentecost and say, "Here; this is it! This is our godly example! The manifestation we practice is identical to the gift of tongues as experienced at Pentecost. We have the Biblical gift of the Spirit."

True?

I wish I could accept their view without further hesitation, but what concerns me is that diligent investigation into the historical background of the phenomena of ecstatic utterings does not come to an abrupt stop upon reaching the Pentecostal experience. The charismatics allude to Pentecost as their supreme example of supernatural tongues; however, the recorded cases of ecstatic speech can be traced as far back as 1100 B.C.; and at the times it occurred prior to the Christian era it was taking place among the heathen tribes inhabiting the Middle East. To them it was a supreme example of possession.

An example of this pre-Christian glossolalia comes to us in a papyrus, now in the Moscow Museum. It dates back to the twenty-first dynasty of Egypt. Written in the colloquial language of the late Egyptian period, it relates the story of Wen-Amon, an official of the temple of Amon at Karnak, who was sent to Byblos in Phoenicia to procure lumber for the construction of a ceremonial barge for the god.

In Byblos, "while he was making offerings to his gods, the god seized one of his youths and made him possessed. And he said to him, 'Bring up [the] god. Bring the messenger who is carrying him! Amon is the one who sent him out! He is the one who made him come!' And while the possessed (youth) was having his frenzy on · this night—" (and the story continues).—*Ancient Near Eastern Texts*, edited by James B.

Pritchard (Princetown, New Jersey: Princetown University Press, 1955), page 26.

This ancient text, historians judge, provides us with the oldest known account of someone becoming possessed and bursting forth with a stream of ecstatic utterances.

Seven hundred years later the renowned Greek philosopher Plato also made mention of the gift of ecstatic speech in his time. In his *Phaedrus*, he demonstrated that he was extremely well acquainted with the phenomenon; for in it he referred to several families who, according to him, were engaged in ecstatic speech, praying and making strange utterings while possessed. Continuing further, he pointed out that these practices even brought physical healing to those who engaged in them. Plato, together with most of his contemporaries, asserted that these occurrences were the result of madness caused by divine inspiration. To support this view, he suggested (in *Timaeus*) that a god takes possession of the mind while man sleeps or is possessed and that during this state the god inspires him with utterances and/or visions which he cannot understand or interpret.

Virgil, too, during the last century before Christ, described in *Aeneid* (Virgil, "Aeneid," trans. James Rhoades, Vol. XIII of *Great Books of the Western World*, ed. R. M. Hutchins, Chicago: Encyclopaedia Brittanica, Inc. 1952, book VI), the activities of the Sybilline priestess on the Island of Delos. He attributed her ecstatic tongues to the result of her being spiritually unified with the god Apollo, a state that enveloped her while she was meditating in the darkness of a haunted cave amidst the eerie sounds of the wind playing strange music through the narrow crevices in the rocks.

In speaking of the Pythoness of Delphi, Chrysostom, the highly acclaimed church father wrote,

"This same Pythoness then is said, being a female, to sit at times upon the tripod of Apollo astride, and thus the *evil spirit* ascending from beneath and entering the lower part of her body, fills the woman with *madness*, and she with disheveled hair begins to play the bachanal and to foam at the mouth, and thus being in a *frenzy* to utter the words of her *madness*."—Chrysostom, "Homilies on First Corinthians," trans. T. W. Chambers, in *The Nicene and Post Nicene Fathers*, ed. Philip Schaff (New York: The Christian Literature Company, 1889) Vol. 12, p. 170. (Italics supplied.)

Many of the so-called mystery religions of the Graeco-Roman world were also undoubtedly using the same phenomena. Among those most often listed are the Osiris cult originating in the land of the Pharaohs; the Mythra cult of the Persians; and the lesser known Eulusinian, Dionysian, and Orphic cults which were cradled in Thrace, Macedonia, and Greece. A thorough study into these religions does not prove conclusively that there was ecstatic speech among them, but experts concur that this was very probably the case. The basis for this opinion is that their entire system of beliefs and rituals was centered around spirit possessions. Another indication comes from Lucian of Samosata (A.D. 120-198) who in *De Dea Syria* describes a clear account of glossolalia as exhibited by an itinerant believer of Juno, the Syrian goddess, stationed at Hierapolis in Syria. (Ira J. Martin, 3rd, *Glossolalia in the Apostolic*

Church [Berea, Ky: Berea College Press, 1960], page 80, cited by Robert G. Gromacki, *The Modern Tongue Movement,* [Philadelphia: Presbyterian and Reformed Publishing Company, 1967], page 8.) It is of interest to note that the term glossolalia, denoting "ecstatic speech," so widely used today, comes from the Greek vernacular which was in existence long before the day of Pentecost.

The Moffatt New Testament Commentary says of these manifestations:

"Oracles of the great 'lord' at the Shrine of Delphi, as Heraclitus put it, were revelations of the god's will through ecstasy, not through sensible words. So were the Sybil's unintelligible cries. A priest or priestess, seized by sudden trances of the spirit, uttered mystic sayings, which were held to be all the more divine as they were least rational or articulate. Philo in Alexandria had taken over the Greek notion, arguing that such ecstasy, when the mind or unconscious reason was superseded, was the highest reach of the human soul in its quest for God."—Comments on 1 Corinthians 14, page 214.

It was in this suffocating atmosphere of heathen superstitions, pagan rituals, devil possession—and, not to be forgotten, Jewish indifference—that Christ was born.

Christ's birth was to be the signal from the Eternal One that the long-awaited period of spiritual restoration for mankind was at hand. The dramatic fall of humanity through the mediumship of a serpent in an earthly paradise, and the apparently irrevocable trend toward an everlasting acceptance of a substitute god suddenly seemed to have been called to a halt. Misunderstood from the start—even by His relatives—Christ slowly moved toward finding acceptance among those He came to rescue. Not being able to comprehend completely the importance of His birth, His disciples soon began to translate His spiritual counsel into mere human values. Believing that He had come to establish an earthly kingdom that would bring an end to the brute force of the merciless Roman Empire, they busied themselves with attempting to divide among themselves the seats of Christ's earthly "cabinet." Overjoyed at the prospect of becoming department heads in the earthly government of Christ, they began to make sly suggestions and hints, with the aim of trying to ascertain which of them would occupy the second highest place in His kingdom, once He had established His government on earth.

Christ labored at the seemingly hopeless task of creating understanding for His mission on earth—and then it happened! Hardened by His admonitions, the Jewish hierarchy, unwilling to accept Him as their long-awaited Messiah, decided on a series of desperate countermoves. Aided by one of His own disciples, they quickly moved in, and, using the Roman occupation powers as executioners, they bloodily erased their only way to salvation, crucifying the King of the universe on a tree of His own creation.

In His wisdom the Son of God had foreseen and foretold this tragic event through His prophets for centuries preceding this cosmic tragedy. But knowing aforehand the effect His death would have on His disciples, He had made provisions to send them a godly replacement.

A *Paraclete*, someone to stand in His place, was what humanity would receive. Devoid of a physical body, this godly "stand-in" would be closer to them and work with them in an even more meaningful way.

In oppressive darkness He uttered the final cries of death to His executioners. Then, when it was all over and the words, "It is finished," were breathed, His dispirited followers stumbled down the hillside, mingling with the bloodthirsty mob.

The subsequent reports of His resurrection built up their hope that all might not be lost, yet it also greatly increased their uneasiness. It was the promise of His godly successor, however, that held them together in their hours of need.

"But ye shall receive power, after that the Holy Ghost is come upon you: and ye shall be witnesses unto me both in Jerusalem, and in all Judea, and in Samaria, and into the uttermost part of the earth." Acts 1:8.

"All power is given unto me in heaven and in earth. Go ye therefore, and teach all nations, baptizing them in the name of the Father, and of the Son, and of the Holy Ghost: teaching them to observe all things whatsoever I have commanded you; and, lo, I am with you alway, even unto the end of the world." Matthew 28:18-20.

Not until a full fifty days after His death did the disciples truly begin to see the significance of His promise.

"And when the day of Pentecost was fully come, they were all with one accord in one place. And suddenly there came a sound from heaven as of a rushing mighty wind, and it filled all the house where they were sitting. And there appeared unto them cloven tongues like as of fire, and it sat upon each of them. And they were all filled with the Holy Ghost, and began to speak

with other tongues, as the Spirit gave them utterance."
Acts 2:1-4.

Among theologians there is hardly any variance in the
interpretation that what happened here dealt with the
ability to speak *real* languages—not a random collection
of unknown sounds.

The term "tongues" (Greek *glōssa*) as used in verse 4
refers to the physical organ used in the art of speaking as
well as to the sound produced by that organ. Also the
word "other" (Greek *heterais*—different) signifies that
the speech produced by the vocal organs of the apostles
consisted of sounds different from those they normally
produced. Verse six of the same chapter furthermore
identifies these *heterais* sounds as distinct languages. The
very wording, *"ēkouon heis hekastos tē idia dialektō
lalountōn autōn* [they kept on hearing them speaking
every one in his own language] ," is sufficient evidence in
itself.

This passage in Acts marks the earliest example of
tongues speaking as a Christian phenomenon, and the
original Greek more than supplies the foundation for the
viewpoint that these sounds were indeed real languages.
What's more, the remainder of the chapter supports this.

"And there were dwelling at Jerusalem Jews, devout
men, out of every nation under heaven. Now when this
was noised abroad, the multitude came together, and
were confounded, because that every man heard them
speak in his own language. And they were all amazed
and marvelled, saying one to another, Behold, are not all
these which speak Galilaeans? And how hear we every
man in our own tongue, wherein we were born?
Parthians, and Medes, and Elamites, and the dwellers in

Mesopotamia, and in Judaea, and Cappadocia, in Pontus, and Asia, Phrygia, and Pamphylia, in Egypt, and in the parts of Libya about Cyrene, and strangers of Rome, Jews and proselytes, Cretes and Arabians, we do hear them speak in our tongues the wonderful works of God. And they were all amazed, and were in doubt, saying one to another, What meaneth this?" Verses 5-12.

This very question is indicative of the fact that they had no conception of the basic philosophy of Christianity, of its power, or of the relationship of this unusual manifestation to the mission Christ had entrusted to His disciples.

Acts 2:5 brings their question into true perspective.

According to law, every devout male Jew living within a twenty-mile radius of Jerusalem was bound to attend the three great yearly Jewish festivals; Passover, Pentecost, and the Feast of Tabernacles. The very word Pentecost indicates that it fell on the fiftieth day after Passover. Since that holiday had already been celebrated in April of that year, Pentecost fell at the beginning of June, one of the most pleasant months in Palestine.

Whereas only the male Jews living within the required distance normally attended the Passover Feast, Pentecost, on the other hand, attracted many more celebrants because of the better traveling conditions which prevailed at that time of year. Undoubtedly thousands of Jews, together with those of Jewish ancestry who had been dispersed throughout the world, returned to Jerusalem to attend the yearly thanksgiving feast, regarding it as a special highlight. Because of their sojourn in distant countries, the majority of them spoke in languages not native to the Holy Land.

Amazed, the foreign travelers now heard these strange Galileans address them in their own language, telling them of the miraculous power of Christ. Relatively unnoticed, unlearned, and born in a part of the Eastern world not necessarily known for its great philosophers, these day laborers and fishermen had suddenly turned into eloquent speakers, conversing with their listeners about the majesty of Christ, reasoning with heavenly wisdom and divinely inspired thoughts. It was indeed an international gathering that surrounded the exuberant apostles who, by now, were thoroughly convinced of the awesome power of the Holy Spirit.

Concerning this event Ellen G. White comments: "Every known tongue was represented by those assembled. This diversity of languages would have been a great hindrance to the proclamation of the gospel; God therefore in a miraculous manner supplied the deficiency of the apostles. The Holy Spirit did for them that which they could not have accomplished for themselves in a lifetime."—*The Acts of the Apostles,* pages 39, 40.

If this was not a miracle, nothing was, and no one in the crowd could ever forget it.

The second example of tongues speaking in connection with the outpouring of the Holy Spirit was equally as impressive, but on this occasion it was given to the Gentiles, not to the Jews. This signified for the first time that Christ's gospel was not reserved exclusively as a saving gesture to the Jewish race, but was intended for the Gentiles as well.

It happened at the house of Cornelius in Caesarea to which Peter had traveled under divine mandate. See Acts 10:17-20.

"While Peter yet spake these words, the Holy Ghost fell on all them which heard the word. And they of the circumcision which believed were astonished, as many as came with Peter, because that on the Gentiles also was poured out the gift of the Holy Ghost. For they heard them speak with tongues, and magnify God." Verses 44-46.

That these men also used actual languages and not a collection of unintelligible sounds is indicated by the words of Scripture which say that Peter and his Jewish brethren heard them "magnify God." Later, referring back to this same event, Peter related: "And as I began to speak, the Holy Ghost fell on them, as on us at the beginning." Acts 11:15. This statement unmistakably identifies their tongues experience with the original Biblical one at Pentecost.

The third time tongues are mentioned in the New Testament is in Acts 19:1-6. Paul, while at Ephesus, had an encounter with twelve disciples of John the Baptist.

"He said unto them, Have ye received the Holy Ghost since ye believed? And they said unto him, We have not so much as heard whether there be any Holy Ghost. And he said unto them, Unto what then were ye baptized? And they said, Unto John's baptism. Then said Paul, John verily baptized with the baptism of repentance, saying unto the people, that they should believe on him which should come after him, that is, on Christ Jesus. When they heard this, they were baptized in the name of the Lord Jesus. And when Paul had laid his hands upon them, the Holy Ghost came on them; and they spake with tongues, and prophesied."

This experience, too, is similar to Pentecost. Taking

into consideration the use of the word *glōssa* in this text, which is the very same word given to describe the other two accounts, would indicate that he did not mean to relate a completely different experience. We may conclude that this, too, was a manifestation of speaking in actual languages, not "unknown tongues."

As far as these three examples of glossolalia are concerned, we seem to be dealing with the supernaturally supplied, God-given ability to speak foreign languages. Because of His gift of glossolalia the early believers could preach the gospel to the known world, providing them with the ultimate means of communication. Apostles and converts embraced it with great enthusiasm.

3

If the passages in Acts were the only Bible references alluding to tongues, there would be little ground for controversy or for the charismatics to speak in unknown sounds. In that case their practice would immediately be recognized as being out of harmony with Biblical guidelines. But Paul's letter to the Corinthians contains passages that have furnished the charismatics with a seemingly firm basis for their position.

What really happened at Corinth?

Let's quickly glance back at the first century and take a look at the background of the church that created all the controversy.

An ancient trading post, Corinth was rebuilt by Julius Caesar as a Roman colony in 46 B.C. Situated between the Ionian and Aegean Seas on the isthmus connecting Greece with the Peloponnesus, and supported by its renowned ports of Lechaeum on the west and Cenchreae on the east, it soon became a major crossroads of Mediterranean commerce. No wonder the emperor selected it to be the Roman capital of the province Achaia, establishing it as the seat of the Roman proconsul.

As a colony of Rome its Greek citizens were also Roman; but other nations were equally well represented —witness the fact that foreign deities such as Isis and Serapis were highly revered with temples nearly as impressive as those of the famed Apollo and Aphrodite. Devil worship and sexual licentiousness were so prevalent and so widely accepted by the Corinthians that Aphrodite's temple alone was staffed by more than 1,000 female slaves solely dedicated to satisfy the lusts of the goddess's earthly subjects.

Realizing all of this, we can see that Paul's efforts to evangelize Corinth could certainly not have been an easy task.

Upon his arrival in Corinth, Paul first lived with Aquila and Priscilla. Acts 18:2. From here he preached to both pagans and Jews. Verse 4. Later Paul left and moved in with Justus, a man whose house was located right next to the Jewish synagogue. Verse 7. His ensuing friendship with Crispus, chief ruler of the synagogue, resulted in the conversion of Crispus's entire household in addition to many other Corinthians.

"Then spake the Lord to Paul in the night by vision, Be not afraid, but speak, and hold not thy peace: For I am with thee, and no man shall set on thee to hurt thee: for I have much people in this city. And he continued there a year and six months, teaching the word of God among them." Acts 18:9-11.

For eighteen difficult months Paul labored there. Then he returned to Syria, leaving behind him the nucleus of a Christian church that was to continue his missionary work among the multitude of nationalities represented in the city.

It was while Paul was in Ephesus on his third missionary journey that the first inklings of trouble among the Corinthian congregation reached him.

Members of Chloe's household first broke the distressing news to Paul. See 1 Corinthians 1:11. Soon afterward it was also reported to him by messenger. See 1 Corinthians 7:1. From these reports Paul became convinced that the church, formed during his second missionary journey and composed chiefly of former Gentiles, had fallen into a bad state of spiritual decomposition. The record of flagrant abuses of Christian living submitted to him were indeed horrifying—not just in number but in degree.

Paul must have been shocked when confronted with the conditions in Corinth. There were, for example, gross division among the Christians, envying, and strife (1 Corinthians 3:3); fornication (5:1); extortioners, and idolators (5:11); court cases involving one Christian against another (6:6); fraud (6:8); association with drunkards, eating food offered to idols (10:19-21); heresies (11:19); attending church in a state of intoxication (11:20, 21); ignorance of spiritual gifts (12:1); denial of the resurrection of the dead (15:12); and abuses of the Lord's Supper (11:27-30).

Is it any wonder that Paul shuddered?

His beloved church had managed to blend once again almost fully with those Corinthian citizens who had made the city famous for its debauchery. They had reverted to paganism, and there seemed no way to check their degeneration. Clearly Christianity had lost its appeal to the former pagans, and with the absence of Paul, there was nothing left to stop their spiritual decline. In fact, to "Corinthianize" had become a byword in the ancient world; and now, instead of being a bright beacon in this dark idolatrous outpost of the Roman Empire, the Corinthian Christian church had practically rejoined the pagans, mocking the power of Christianity.

While these violations are duly noted and rebuked in the first letter to the Corinthians, Paul devotes much attention to the improper handling of the gift of speaking in tongues. *It must be stated, however, that nowhere in the letter does Paul speak out against the tongues or suggest that the Corinthians were engaged in practicing a counterfeit manifestation. In fact, Paul wants all the believers in Corinth to "speak with tongues," saying expressly that he does "not forbid speaking with tongues." He also thanked God, stating, "I speak with tongues more than ye all." 1 Corinthians 14:5, 39, 18.*

This combination of statements by Paul indicates that

he held the Corinthian tongues to be valid manifestations of godly glossolalia, not a devilish counterfeit. Would he, a man of God, have uttered the wish that "all speak with tongues" if the practice had been spurious? Would he have counseled them not to "forbid speaking with tongues" or admitted that he spoke "with tongues more than ye all"?

It is incomprehensible to imagine Paul *not* forbidding them to "speak with tongues" if what they practiced was the heathen counterfeit of the true gift of tongues. Also could we imagine Paul wanting all the believers to speak in tongues if this referred to the counterfeit manifestation? As for Paul's claim, "I speak with tongues more than ye all," would he have said this if they had indeed been involved in practicing ungodly glossolalia? Why, using the language of the twentieth century, would Paul have said, "I speak more types of gibberish than you do," knowing that the pagan counterfeit was not the identical experience of that at Pentecost?

It would have been most incongruous indeed!

Chapters 12, 13, and 14 of the first book of Corinthians deal with tongues; and even a cursory glance shows that it provides rules for an orderly use of this gift of the Spirit; it does not pronounce a condemnation of the basic experience.

Paul's strong stand in regard to the tongues manifestation in the Corinthian church has spawned many different interpretations of Corinthians 12, 13, and 14. Some, after studying all available evidence, conscientiously arrive at the conclusion that even though Paul did not expressly forbid speaking in tongues, he nevertheless cautioned seriously against the use of the Corinthian manifestation as it was basically a counterfeit as compared to Paul's usage of real, intelligent foreign languages. Others are convinced that it was neither counterfeit nor use of intelligent foreign languages, but a manifestation of a godly ecstatic utterance, bearing no resemblance to either.

Many researchers, however, believe that both Paul and the Corinthians used supernaturally supplied foreign languages, and that Paul's letter to the degenerate Corinthian church was intended to teach them the correct usage of these godly tongues.

I hold the latter position, for a study of this New Testament phenomenon does not furnish us with proof or indications, no matter how vague, that the godly gift of tongues had been changed from a manifestation of speaking real languages (as in Acts 2:1-4) to unintelligible sounds by the time it was being used by the Corinthians. To the contrary, it seems reasonable to assume that inasmuch as Corinth was a city with a cosmopolitan populace because of its role in being the political and commercial hub of the province of Achaia, its citizenry was composed of a great variety of nationalities, supplemented with a constant influx of commercial travelers. When Paul established the church at Corinth, it seems probable that its members received the gift of tongues in order to reach out to all of these resident aliens and itinerant foreigners in their own language.

Paul admits as much.

"That in every thing ye are enriched by him, in all utterance, and (in) all knowledge," he points out in his letter. "Even as the testimony of Christ was confirmed in you: so that ye come behind in no gift; waiting for the coming of our Lord Jesus Christ." 1 Corinthians 1:5, 6.

After listing the problems that infiltrated the Corinthian church in the first eleven chapters of his letter to the troubled congregation, Paul finally arrives at the problem area. He says, "Now concerning spiritual gifts, brethren, I would not have you ignorant." "Now there are diversities of gifts, but the same Spirit." 1 Corinthians 12:1, 4.

"For to one is given by the Spirit the word of wisdom; to another the word of knowledge by the same Spirit; to another faith by the same Spirit; to another the gifts of healing by the same Spirit; to another the working of miracles; to another prophecy; to another discerning of spirits; to another divers kinds of tongues; to another the interpretation of tongues." Verses 8-10.

Paul obviously knew that the Corinthians possessed unwholesome views concerning the gifts of the Spirit. He compares it to ignorance! The entire list of complaints he had received indicated that the church had drifted toward heathenism, and the fact that Paul devotes two complete chapters to the tongues proves that the use of this godly gift especially had fallen into disrepute. It would have been remarkable indeed if the church, having already plunged neck-deep in paganism and having ignored God's guidance in everything else, had in some way managed to preserve the gift of tongues unblemished; for most of these Christians had a heathen background, where speaking in tongues was held in high esteem and was regarded as a token of favor from the gods.

Commenting on this, Edward Schweizer writes:

"In Corinth a conception of the Spirit of God was predominant with mixed-up Holy Spirit and enthusiasm. To the Corinthians, an utterance seemed to be more godly the more miraculous it appeared. Thus glossolalia was the highest degree of spiritual maturity, just because it showed itself depending on a mysterious power which would not be identified with any natural faculty of man."—"The Service of Worship," *Interpretation,* October, 1959, p. 403.

The ability to speak other languages had been bestowed by God as an express means to evangelize the world, and the emphasis Paul gives it shows that this gift had become a subject of much controversy.

Setting himself squarely in the center of the conflict, he deflates the importance the Corinthians had placed on the gift. To them it had always been the supreme proof of godliness, and because of its role in early Christianity, it attracted many converts.

These believers came from the mystery religions. A new religion led by a God who had become a man, who could cast out devils, heal the sick, raise the dead, multiply food, make wine out of water, and walk on water—to such converts this was the ultimate. What's more, not only did this God Himself come back to life after having been cruelly murdered, but He ascended to heaven in plain sight of a group of His followers!

What they lacked in conviction, they compensated for with their eagerness to be one with this "new" God. To many of them Paul's message must have seemed to be the utmost in mystery religions. There is no question that a great number of members of the early Corinthian church joined because of faith in Christ; but others undoubtedly joined because of the supernatural appeal. Does it not seem reasonable to presume that because of this the gift of tongues had begun to occupy such a prominent position in the church? But now Paul moves in and gives it an entirely different place.

Twice in his admonishing letter to the Corinthians, Paul lists the various spiritual gifts, both times ending it with tongues and interpretation, which was understandably a shock to the Corinthians.

In 1 Corinthians 12:8-10, he mentions seven gifts, and then, almost as an afterthought, he adds the gifts of tongues and interpretation. That this was done intentionally seems obvious when comparing it to the second list in 1 Corinthians 12:28-30. Here again he lists seven gifts and again tongues and interpretation come last of all. In the lists of spiritual gifts given in Romans 12:6-8 and Ephesians 4:7-11 they are not mentioned at all.

The gifts of tongues and interpretation are distinguished from the other gifts of the spirit by their communicative qualities. *They were gifts of communication.* Through the gift of tongues—the ability to speak other languages—the apostles were able to transmit the knowledge and beauty of God to other nations in their own languages; the gift of interpretation was given to enable them to carry on a dialogue, an intelligent conversation with those speaking other languages; for this gift enabled them to understand those who spoke in other tongues. By ranking the other spiritual gifts before those of tongues and interpretation, Paul practically says that the knowledge of God's revelations received by the Christians through the first five gifts is to be relayed to others through the last two gifts; for without divine thoughts and ideas to communicate, the gifts of tongues and interpretation have no value.

When Paul therefore asked, "Are all apostles? are all prophets? are all teachers? are all workers of miracles? have all the gifts of healing? do all speak with tongues? do all interpret?" 1 Corinthians 12:29, 30, he apparently had a reason for this repetitious text.

In the final verse of the chapter he gives the answer.

"But covet earnestly the best gifts; and yet shew I unto you a more excellent way." Verse 31.

In Paul's opinion, the gifts so highly revered by the Corinthians—tongues and their interpretation—were not really so important. Plainly he advises them here to seek the gift with the greatest value for the church—that of prophecy. Verse 5 of chapter 14 substantiates this:

"I would that ye all spake with tongues, but rather that ye prophesied: for greater (is) he that prophesieth than he that speaketh with tongues, except he interpret, that the church may receive edifying."

Thus the Corinthians had indeed placed the wrong emphasis on tongues and were misusing them. Rather than seeking a gift that would edify the church, they sought for a manifestation that would edify themselves, (verse 4) and in so doing they were destroying the church.

There are Bible scholars who hold the view that God would never allow a person to misuse a godly gift. "What happened in Corinth," they argue, "must have been ecstatic utterance, for God would never allow a church that had retreated that far from His principles to retain one of His precious gifts."

It is a point worth considering.

Imagine, for a moment, that you or I would be caught (by God) fondly gazing upon some of the modern literature considered by the U.S. Supreme Court to be obscene. Would we expect God to come down in wrath and destroy our gift of sight? To give another example, if we were observed overhearing a conversation we should not have been interested in or listening to jokes outside the realm of decency, would we expect God to destroy our gift of hearing?

At birth, we have all received certain natural gifts from God. Sight, hearing, touch, smell, reason—they are all precious gifts which we retain until we die unless disease or accident steps in. Yet, when we use these gifts for nongodly purposes, God does not punish us immediately by taking these gifts away from us; rather, He reserves His punishment until the day of accounting, when our sins and violations will be measured against our knowledge and understanding of God's principles and His laws. Would not God thus delay judgment, in much this same way, for misuse of the gift of tongues? God did not immediately remove the gift of prophecy from Balaam, the rebellious prophet. See Numbers, chapters 22-24.

God gave the Corinthians the supernatural ability to speak intelligent foreign languages, enabling them to reach other nationalities. This gift was a godly extension of the human gift of speech. When the Corinthians began to lose their close fellowship with God by embracing once again some of the major doctrines of paganism, their responsibility to Him increased sharply—for they knew better. Thus, when they continued to use the gift of tongues for self edification—attempting to impress others that they "had to be godly" since they spoke with other tongues, while in reality they were no longer recipients of God's blessings through the other five gifts—He did not strike them dumb or take away their language ability. No. He merely added this violation to the others and held them responsible for this misuse of a godly gift.

Only God knows how seriously He will regard this violation. Only the final judgment will tell.

It had become necessary for Paul to give some hard counsel, and he didn't hesitate to do so. Realizing that the gift of tongues in Corinth had become a communication medium without substance (for how would they be able to transmit the beauty of the gospel and the immense love of Christ if they themselves had lost the concept of its very meaning and were living in open violation of supreme love?), he lectured them with some straightforward talk.

"Though I speak with the tongues of men and of angels, and have not charity, I am become as sounding brass, or a tinkling cymbal." Then he continued, "Charity suffereth long, and is kind; charity envieth not; charity vaunteth not itself, is not puffed up, doth not behave itself unseemly, seeketh not her own, is not easily provoked, thinketh no evil; rejoiceth not in iniquity, but rejoiceth in the truth; beareth all things, believeth all things, hopeth all things, endureth all things." 1 Corinthians 13:1, 4-7. Then, after pointing out the superiority of charity, he advised, "Follow after charity, and desire spiritual gifts, but rather that ye may prophesy." 1 Corinthians 14:1.

Many Bible translators have throughout the years substituted the word "love" for "charity." Paul advises the believers to reach out for those qualities that would make it impossible for them to tolerate the conditions they had brought into the church—the very ones which caused him to write the letter.

Paul does not claim (in 1 Corinthians 13:1) that he speaks with the tongues of men and of angels. Dr. Gerhard F. Hasel of Andrews University correctly suggests that, "Paul seems to say with hyperbole that if all linguistic possibilities including divine speech were at his disposal and he lacked love, it would mean nothing." Then he states emphatically: "First Corinthians 13:1 does not provide the key to Paul's idea of 'speaking in tongues.' "—*The New Testament Teaching on "Speaking in Tongues,"* page 69. (Presented at the Study Conference on the Charismatic Movement.)

Kenneth Taylor, in *The Living Bible, Paraphrased*, gives 1 Corinthians 13:1 as follows:

"If I had the gift of being able to speak in other languages without learning them, and could speak in every language there is in all of heaven and earth, but didn't love others, I would only be making noise."

At this point it would be well for us to recognize the subtle changes translators have brought about in the Bible. Throughout Paul's discussion of the manifestation of tongues in chapters 12, 13, and 14 of 1 Corinthians he used the word "tongue" or "tongues" twenty-three times. Oddly enough, in verses 2, 4, 14, 19, and 27 of chapter 14 the adjective "unknown" precedes the "tongue" or "tongues." Nowhere can this be found in the original text! The translators who prepared the King

James Version merely added it to the texts with the hope that it would help to clarify the meaning. This is signified in many editions, particularly older ones, by printing the word in italics.

It appears now that they have accomplished just the opposite.

Chapter 14 provides most of the statements used by glossolalists in their attempts to form a sound basis for their position, beginning with the first verse and continuing almost uninterruptedly through to verse forty.

Notice the wording of verses 2-5 with the supplied words in parenthesis:

"For he that speaketh in an (unknown) tongue speaketh not unto men, but unto God: for no man understandeth (him); howbeit in the spirit he speaketh mysteries. But he that prophesieth speaketh unto men (to) edification, and exhortation, and comfort. He that speaketh in an (unknown) tongue edifieth himself; but he that prophesieth edifieth the church. I would that ye all spake with tongues, but rather that ye prophesied: for greater (is) he that prophesieth than he that speaketh with tongues, except he interpret, that the church may receive edifying."

Considering the many languages spoken in Corinth because of its cosmopolitan nature, certain members of the congregation undoubtedly were able to converse fluently in more than one "tongue" because of their association with foreigners. Also, there must have been many who had received the "gift of tongues" supernaturally.

"Do you speak a language?" is a question often asked Americans of foreign extraction, not with the intent of inquiring into their ability to speak English but rather if they can speak a foreign language or a foreign tongue. When someone queries, "How many languages do you speak?" he most certainly does not want to know whether the subject speaks English. That's rather obvious. He wants to know how many other languages, and this is precisely the issue in the Corinthian letter.

When Paul states, "He that speaketh in a . . . tongue speaketh not unto men, but unto God," he is simply saying that if you speak with a tongue or language in church (that he is speaking of activities within the church is indicated in the remainder of the chapter), you really only speak to God, for no one else understands it. In other words he says, "In the spirit he speaketh mysteries."

"Prophesy!" he exclaims. At least that edifies the church. The speaker in tongues, on the other hand, only edifies himself, that is, makes himself look important, since he himself is his only listener.

Somewhat attempting to soften his approach, but not without failing to emphasize his position once again, he states (paraphrased), I wish you would all speak in languages, but I'd prefer that you'd prophesy, for that is far superior to speaking in languages unless you have it interpreted so that it may benefit the church. Paul does not forbid foreigners to use their languages in the church, but strongly desires their comments to be translated for the good of the church. Does it not seem reasonable to assume that here Paul is specifically speaking to people who were employing the gift of glossolalia incorrectly within the church instead of using it to evangelize Corinth? Perhaps others were using a learned language within the church to make it appear that they too had received a gift from the Spirit; or some may have used their native (foreign) tongue in worship services. Inasmuch as they had a common language, there was no apparent need for "tongues" within the church—hence Paul's admonition.

In verse 6 Paul goes a step farther:

"Now, brethren, if I come unto you speaking with tongues, what shall I profit you, except I shall speak to you either by revelation, or by knowledge, or by prophesying, or by doctrine?"

Simple but straightforward counsel! Paul undoubtedly used many diverse languages on his missionary journeys, but how would it benefit the church if he should come to them speaking in tongues they were unable to understand. And then Paul makes a comparison intended to erase all possible misconceptions.

"And even things without life giving sound, whether pipe or harp, except they give a distinction in the sounds, how shall it be known what is piped or harped? For if the trumpet give an uncertain sound, who shall prepare himself to the battle? So likewise ye, except ye utter by the tongue words easy to be understood, how shall it be known what is spoken? for ye shall speak into the air." Verses 7-9.

His reference to trumpet sounds during battle is especially meaningful. Even as recent as the last century commands to retreat or attack were given by trumpet or bugle. Only when these sounds were distinct and clear could their true meaning be understood by the armies. Confusing sounds would meet with disastrous results. Once again Paul cautions against the use of sounds other than normally used—"for ye shall speak into the air."

Paul gives another example:

"There are, it may be, so many kinds of voices in the world, and none of them (is) without signification. Therefore if I know not the meaning of the voice, I shall be unto him that speaketh a barbarian, and he that speaketh (shall be) a barbarian unto me." Verses 10, 11.

Some Bible translations (such as RSV, NAS, TEV, Phillips, Weymouth, Goodspeed, and Moffatt) have translated the original word used for "voices" as "languages," a meaning wholeheartedly endorsed by many New Testament scholars. Consequently, what Paul in actuality is referring to is that there are many languages in the world; but without knowing what the speaker is saying, both speaker and hearer will be as strangers to one another. By saying this, he attempts to point out once more the absurdity of their actions.

Next Paul speaks to those in the church who had the ability to speak either supernaturally supplied or intellectually learned languages:

"Wherefore let him that speaketh in an (unknown) tongue pray that he may interpret. For if I pray in an (unknown) tongue, my spirit prayeth, but my understanding is unfruitful. What is it, then? I will pray with the spirit, and I will pray with the understanding also: I will sing with the spirit, and I will sing with the understanding also." Verses 13-15.

Different meanings can be attached to verse 13. Perhaps Paul means that someone who speaks in a language should pray that someone else in the congregation may receive the ability to interpret him. Or it could mean that he should pray that someone else might receive the power to explain what he had just been saying. Verse 14 points to the first conclusion, for Paul compares it to a prayer uttered in a language; he goes on to state that in such case the spirit prays but the action of the mind produces no results, no fruits, and is thus "unfruitful."

In corporate worship, public prayer is offered to God as an expression of love—the devotion of the entire congregation. If spoken, however, in a "foreign" language, its function as part of the corporate worship ceases. Then in verse 15 Paul ties both the "spirit" and the "understanding" together. Commented Dr. Walter Specht, a New Testament scholar and theologian at Andrews University, Berrien Springs, Michigan: "He who preaches the sermon in a worship service is speaking for God to the people. He who offers the prayer is speaking for the people to God. It requires an intelligent exercise of the mind as well as the spirit to meet this sacred responsibility."

Both spirit and understanding are needed for an intelligent communication in praying and in singing. Paul adds that if one prays with the spirit alone while in the company of the "unlearned" it won't give them a reason to say "amen" because they will not be able to understand the meaning of the sound they hear. Public response to a prayer has always been important. The word "amen," Hebrew for "so be it," is a standard ending to a Christian prayer, and when members of a congregation join in a corporate prayer and make it their own, they signify this by repeating this word. Yet how could this be done if the language used in the prayer was unintelligible?

Says Paul, speaking of this type of prayer, "For thou verily givest thanks well, but the other is not edified." 1 Corinthians 14:17.

Glossolalists invariably quote verse 18 of chapter 14 as "proof" that even Paul himself spoke in unknown tongues.

Let's see what Paul did say: "I thank my God, I speak with tongues more than ye all: yet in the church I had rather speak five words with my understanding, that (by my voice) I might teach others also, than ten thousand words in an (unknown) tongue." Verses 18, 19.

Paul was a world traveler. Especially endowed with the Holy Spirit, leader of a God-directed missionary movement, he journeyed from country to country, conversing with other nationalities in their native tongues. Would God limit Paul's gift of tongues to only one foreign language? Personally I don't want to set any limitations on the power of God at all! Knowing Christ's desire to spread the gospel to all the world, I do not doubt that Paul really meant that he had the ability to speak with more languages than all the others. His God entrusted him with a commission unequaled in scope and importance, and He would definitely not confine this great task to only one foreign language area. To allude that verse 18 indicates that Paul spoke in many different kinds of gibberish is accusing God of creating confusion, yet, "God is not (the author) of confusion, but of peace, as in all churches of the saints." Verse 33.

Furthermore, in verse 19 Paul explains that, even though he speaks many languages, he would rather speak five words with understanding than ten thousand in an unknown language. Then in verse 22 he makes a clear distinction between the roles tongues and prophecy are to play in the church:

"Wherefore tongues are for a sign, not to them that believe, but to them that believe not: but prophesying (serveth) not for them that believe not, but for them which believe." Don't demonstrate your language ability to fellow believers, he counsels here, but reserve it for the unbelievers to show them that God has given you a special blessing which enables you to preach to them in their own language. Don't bring your tongues into the church but prophesy instead, for that is given for the benefit of the believers.

Then he goes on to discuss a point which no doubt had been in the center of the controversy: "If therefore the whole church be come together into one place, and all speak with tongues, and there come in (those that are) unlearned, or unbelievers, will they not say that ye are mad?" Verse 23.

And a few verses later he comes to the problem again: "How is it then, brethren? when ye come together, every one of you hath a psalm, hath a doctrine, hath a tongue, hath a revelation, hath an interpretation. Let all things be done unto edifying." Verse 26.

Imagine the chaos that must have prevailed within the Corinthian church! One group speaking foreign languages, other members vying for attention to propagate a new doctrine, others claiming to have a revelation or to interpret tongues, while perhaps a few true Christians prayed in quiet meditation. It is no wonder that Paul questioned, "Will they not say that ye are mad?" A spiritual chaos such as this can never be edifying, and his admonishment, "Let all things be done unto edifying," was more than necessary. The situation confronting Paul unquestionably turned unbelievers away from the church, and this he wanted to avoid at all costs.

Deeply troubled, Paul established guidelines under which the Corinthian church would be allowed to practice their spiritual gifts. Normally this counsel would not be needed, as mature Christians would not consciously misuse a gift of God. However, the Corinthians' immaturity in spiritual matters necessitated some strict rules, and these Paul proceeded to provide:

"If any man speak in an (unknown) tongue, (let it be) by two, or at the most (by) three, and (that) by course; and let one interpret. But if there be no interpreter, let him keep silence in the church; and let him speak to himself, and to God. Let the prophets speak two or three, and let the other judge. If (any thing) be revealed to another that sitteth by, let the first hold his peace. For ye may all prophesy one by one, that all may learn, and all may be comforted." Verses 27-31.

Paul does not forbid speaking in tongues, nor does he prohibit prophesying. He does insist, however, that if there are those who speak in a language, then let them do it one at a time and only then if an interpreter is present. If this is not the case, then let them speak only to God, i.e. without involving the congregation. He laid down basically the same rules for the prophets. Prophesying was to be done by one to teach and to comfort. This certainly sounds reasonable, doesn't it? Speak in tongues one by one only if there is someone who can translate, and prophesy one by one and let the others judge, using the gift to teach and comfort the church. Nowhere does Paul advocate that tongues are to be spoken within the church nor that prophesying was to be proclaimed outside of the church, neither does he give any indication that the tongues he was describing had undergone a change in linguistic structure since Pentecost.

Paul concludes his discussion on tongues with some emphatic exhortations: "If any man think himself to be a prophet, or spiritual, let him acknowledge that the things that I write unto you are the commandments of the Lord. But if any man be ignorant, let him be ignorant. Wherefore, brethren, covet to prophesy, and forbid not to speak with tongues. Let all things be done decently and in order." Verses 37-40.

And with those final injunctions Paul closed his message to the members whose indecent behavior had brought discredit upon the church and whose disorderly conduct had greatly impeded its growth.

An interesting point arises whenever scholars congregate to discuss the gifts of the Spirit and the misconceptions held within the Corinthian church in connection with these gifts.

Even though most theologians have basically the same background and many of them have received their degrees from the same universities or seminaries, many feel that they can make a genuine contribution to Bible interpretation if in some way they are able to arrive at a new, plausible explanation of a text that has thus far presented problems.

I have attended several sessions where the gift of tongues was discussed, and as a nontheologian I have stood amazed at the differences in opinion.

One theologian told me that the reason Paul's counsel

to the Corinthians might appear confused is that he was confronted with a problem with which he was unacquainted. "He didn't know what to tell them," I was told, "and consequently he was not too clear."

Now if one thing is obvious, it is that Paul was rarely at a loss for words. By just reading his letter to the Romans we have ample evidence that he was a master wordsmith, using words in such a manner as to transmit what he meant to say. Why should he have acted differently when giving counsel to a church on the verge of spiritual death? He had established the Corinthian church as a major focal point of missionary activity, and he was now working in a heathen world where ungodly glossolalia was still prevalent. Are we to believe that Paul would have been confronted with a phenomenon for which he had no answer?

Paul is deep—but never confused. When he wrote the letter to the Corinthians, rebuking them for their misuse of the godly gift, he was as straightforward as he could be. He did not hide behind uninterpretable adjectives; he did not deal in metaphors, nor did he deluge his readers with parables. He counseled them in a forthright manner and told them how to correct their error.

Paul gave no hint to the Corinthians that they should try to figure out what he really meant. It is this frankness, this openness, this certainty that gives me the distinct feeling that Paul's letter to them was not meant to be examined for hidden meanings. Rather, it was written to be read for reproof and rebuke in the way it was given—not to be treated as a philosophical discourse.

It is this constant search for a "new meaning" within the words Paul penned to the Corinthians that is causing confusion. Not Paul's counsel.

During the first few centuries following the death of Christ, the Pentecostal experience of the apostles as recorded in the book of Acts, became an accepted practice. In the beginning were the apostles, next their converts, who continued to carry the gospel to far distant lands. In later years it allowed whole countries to be exposed to the revolutionary message of love, either by missionaries or by natives who relayed the story of Christ to their home countries. As a result, the need for speaking in tongues diminished, for language was no longer a serious barrier. This obstacle to the spreading of the gospel had been surmounted.

I believe that a diligent examination of those early century historians supports the view that the gift of tongues had been given to humanity only to do a specific job.

Significant comments on 1 Corinthians 2:6 were made by the ultra-orthodox church father Irenaeus (A.D. c. 130-c. 202). A scholar of stature, he studied under Polycarp of Smyrna, who is reported to have been a personal protégé of the apostle John.

In "Against Heresies," Irenaeus wrote: "Terming those persons 'perfect' who have received the Spirit of God, and who through the Spirit of God do speak in all languages, as he used Himself also to speak. In like manner we do also hear many brethren in the Church who possess prophetic gifts, and who through the Spirit speak all kinds of languages and bring to light for the general benefit the hidden things of men, and declare the mysteries of God."—"Against Heresies," Bk. V, ch. vi. In *The Ante-Nicene Fathers*, eds. Alexander Roberts and

James Donaldson, (New York: Charles Scribner's Sons, 1899), Vol. 1, p. 531.

The Christian apologist, Justin Martyr (A.D. c. 100-c. 165) supports this in his "Dialogue With Trypho," page 88, where he states, "Now it is possible to see amongst us women and men who possess gifts of the Spirit of God."

Even Tertullian (A.D. c. 160-c. 220) writes concerning his acquaintanceship with the gift. In his argument with Marcion he penned the following statement:

"Let Marcion then exhibit, as gifts of his god, some prophets, such as have not spoken by human sense, but with the Spirit of God, such as have both predicted things to come, and have made manifest the secrets of the heart; let him produce a psalm, a vision, a prayer— only let it be by the spirit, in an ecstasy, that is, in a rapture, whenever an interpretation of tongues has occurred to him. . . . Now all these signs (of spiritual gifts) are forthcoming from my side without any difficulty, and they agree, too, with the rules, and the dispensations, and the instructions of the Creator; therefore without doubt the Christ, and the Spirit, and the apostle, belong severally to my God."—"Tertullian Against Marcion," Bk. V, ch. viii, in *The Ante-Nicene Fathers,* Vol. 3, pp. 446, 447.

There was every reason to keep the gift of tongues active so long as the gospel had not reached the strategic locations of the known world. Once this was accomplished and considerable inroads had been made, the gift of tongues diminished.

It was not until the fourth century after Christ that scholars and historians began to question the whereabouts of the preaching tongues.

Discussing the spiritual gifts as found in 1 Corinthians, John Chrysostom (A.D. c. 345-407) wrote:

"This whole place is very obscure [referring to 1 Corinthians 12:1, 2], but the obscurity is produced by our ignorance of the facts referred to and by their cessation, being such as then used to occur but now no longer take place."

Was this perhaps the crucial point where the gift of tongues had done its work and had been retracted by God? There is no reason to doubt the validity of Chrysostom's statement, more so since Augustine (A.D. 354-430) reaches practically the same conclusion. "In the earliest time, 'the Holy Ghost fell upon them that believed, and they spake with tongues,' which they had not learned, 'as the Spirit gave them utterance.' These were signs adapted to the times," Augustine pointed out. "For there behooved to be that betokening of the Holy Spirit in all tongues, to shew that the Gospel of God was to run through all tongues over the whole earth. That thing was done for a betokening, and it passed away."—"Ten Homilies on the First Epistle of John," Homily VI, sec. 10, in *The Nicene and Post-Nicene Fathers,* ed. Philip Schaff (New York: The Christian Literature Company, 1888), Vol. 7, pp. 497, 498.

Some theologians have tried to build a case for a continuation of the supernatural languages on the basis of an isolated questionable example (Montanus). However, the true gift of tongues, after having been manifested in strength in the apostolic age and possibly to the third century, faded from the scene. I do not know of any historian since that time who has uncovered any concrete evidence to the contrary. If it had remained within the church, writings of other church fathers of those early centuries would have without question referred to this "gift of the Spirit" in glowing terms as it was a major manifestation of God-power. The gift was so controversial and so clearly supernatural from its very inception that a continuation of it could scarcely have gone unnoticed or unreported.

True speaking in tongues disappeared because of its decreasing need. But what about the useless gibberish, the senseless syllables used by the pagans?

The occult practitioners maintain that it *never* disappeared but remained active within the coves of the witches, the magicians' caves, and the seance rooms of the mediums. Theirs was the Satanic counterfeit, for God would never manifest Himself in this manner within their circles. Even then their gift apparently lay more or less dormant until a full thousand years after Christ. Then a woman, Hildegard, Prophet of the Rhine (1098-1179) forced it back into the limelight.

The Catholic Encyclopedia, in describing her "Lingua Ignota," a manuscript relating her experiences, states as follows:

"The manuscript in eleven folios, . . . gives a list of nine hundred words of an unknown language, mostly nouns and only a few adjectives, a Latin, and in a few cases a German, explanation, together with an unknown alphabet of twenty-three letters, printed in Pitra."—*The Catholic Encyclopedia* (New York: The Encyclopedia Press, Inc., 1913), Vol. VII, p. 352, art. "Hildegard." If this was true glossolalia, a drastic transformation must have taken place over the centuries of silence, for her sounds were strange and weird, without any comparison to either a known language or a language structure. It has received careful scrutiny from various linguists, but no one has been able to make it "fit." In fact, no one has been able to make it match certain norms to which all languages—if they are to be mediums of communication—must conform.

Much of modern glossolalia had its beginnings in the post-Reformation era. Granted, Martin Luther did not practice the gift personally—neither in its legitimate nor in its illegitimate fashion—but the many cults and sects which his movement spawned soon felt the need for "exclusive" experiences and unique methods which would guarantee them their continuing contact with God on a highly personal level. The uncertainty which prevailed in the sixteenth and seventeenth centuries was undoubtedly a major reason for this search for exclusiveness and spiritual superiority.

Together with the more formal doctrines, speaking in tongues crept in and became an accepted rite in many worship services of the new sects. Again the start was rather slow, but once the strange utterances had been judged to be of divine origin, they occurred in the weirdest places.

William Howitt, in *History of the Supernatural*, describes a happening in Amsterdam in 1566 as follows:

"They climbed up the walls and over roofs like cats, made the most horrible grimaces, and spoke in foreign languages. . . . Sometimes they became cataleptic, were stiff as trunks of trees, and might be carried about in the same manner."

The Jansenists, named after their founder Cornelis

Jansen, were members of a seventeenth century Catholic reform movement known also for their ecstatic behavior. They too exhibited glossolalia, usually while meditating at the tomb of the Archdeacon of Paris, a staunch defender of Jansenism. Convulsive movements, tongues, and other physical signs which resulted from their meditative actions convinced them that the Spirit of God was with them. It is significant that they believed—as do modern glossolalists—that an outside power controlled their speech organs and compelled them to utter words and convulsive signs over which they had no control.

The case of "Mother" Ann Lee, (1736-1784), founder of the Shakers, focused the attention of the religious world of the eighteenth century on a renewed emphasis on tongues. Even prior to her coming to the United States, "Mother" Lee had already experienced her share of trouble in England because of her highly erratic behavior. Accused of blasphemy, she was summoned to explain her actions before a group of clergymen-linguists of the Church of England. While appearing before them, she received her "gift" of the spirit and proceeded to speak to the assembled clergymen in no less than seventy-two different languages—at least that's what they claimed. A number of them went even further to state that she spoke many of these languages fluently. The question here, of course, is where on earth did the Church of England manage to find four ministers who were expertly qualified to judge the grammatical accuracy of seventy-two distinctly different languages. George W. Dollar, in referring to the Shakers' other expressions of spiritual ecstasy, writes,

"The gift of tongues was also accompanied by times of unspeakable joy and dancing during which many of the hymns of the movement were composed, although made up of unintelligible and unheard of words."—George W. Dollar, "Church History of the Tongues Movement," *Bibliotheca Sacra*, October-December 1963, p. 320.

Begging for attention are two other examples of untranslatable gibberish—that of the Irvingites and the Mormons. The former, operating in Britain as followers of the Scotch Presbyterian Edward Irving, evidenced a strong apocalyptic interest and became convinced that the gift of tongues would be returned to the church before the soon second coming of Christ. Strange sounds began to emanate from the mouths of the worshipers. Interpretations that followed classified the expressions as both languages and gibberish. In the opinion of R. A. Knox, its linguistic value is indeed questionable. He writes in *Enthusiam* (London, 1950, p. 553) that "specimens of Irvingite glossolaly which have been preserved to us are beyond the reach of any lexicon. Such utterances of 'Hippo gerosto niparos boorastin farini O fastor sungor boorinos epoongos menati? . . . ' hardly bear out the claim that 'the languages are distinct, well-inflected, well-compacted languages.' The philology of another world does not abide our question, but if we are to judge these results by merely human standards, we must admit that a child prattles no less convincingly."

As for the Mormons, founded by Joseph Smith (1805-1844), the principle of speaking in tongues was first introduced by him into his church in 1833 and reaffirmed in a declaration of Mormon doctrines eleven years later. It must be said, however, that the early

Mormons never claimed that what was spoken was indeed a language. They did declare though that God would shape the various sounds into a language and make it meaningful.

Referring to one of those meetings, it has been reported that "it would be advertised that at a certain meeting someone would speak with tongues. When the meeting was well under way, Father Smith would call upon some illiterate brother to rise and speak in tongues in the name of Jesus Christ.

"The order was given, 'Arise upon your feet, speak or make some sound, continue to make sounds of some kind, and the Lord will make a tongue or language of it.' "—C. B. Cutten, *Speaking in Tongues,* page 68.

The truth is that glossolalia did not start with Pentecost—nor did it end there. The true gift of languages disappeared when God saw no further necessity for its use, but the counterfeit persisted. History speaks quite plainly when it comes to supplying examples of pagan glossolalia in pre-Christian times. The introduction of a true gift of languages in Acts only furnished the counterfeit with a new impetus. It now made it possible for its advocates to confuse the issue by comparing "their" gift to the God-given ability, thus shedding wherever possible its heathen heritage, enshrouding its post-Christian continuation of the phenomenon with a cloak of Christian respectability.

There would be no controversy concerning the gift of tongues and its role in the twentieth century churches if the "experts" could agree that the tongues of the glossolalists are indeed real languages. They don't, and it has set tempers flaring.

Attempting to clarify their views, the charismatics often use learned scholars backed by impressive credentials to substantiate their stand. And the conservatives do the same.

The basic problem is the establishment of the precise meaning of the word "language." Webster's *New International Dictionary* (Second Edition) has defined the word, but has not removed all difficulty. Webster defines "language" as follows:

"Audible, articulate human speech as produced by the action of the tongue and adjacent vocal organs. . . . The body of words and methods of combining words used and understood by a considerable community, esp. when fixed and elaborated by long usage. . . . In the usual sense, *language* means a system of conventionalized signs, esp. words or gestures having fixed meaning."

Taking this definition for a ground rule, it appears

that no matter where or when a language is spoken, to be classified as such it must be understood by a large number of people; it has to be of such uniformity that it can be learned; it must have a grammatical structure and can therefore not be untranslatable or full of hidden meaning.

"Not so," says Howard M. Erwin of the Graduate School of Theology of the Oral Roberts University in Tulsa, Oklahoma.

"When we speak our native tongue, we speak the words that are in our minds, words that in choice, inflection, nuance and color manifest our personalities. When we speak in 'tongues,' as the Holy Spirit gives utterance, we speak those words that are in the mind of the Spirit, words that manifest his personality unfettered by the censorship of the human ego. These words are, therefore, an exquisitely personal self-manifestation of the Holy Spirit."—"As the Spirit Gives Utterance," *Christianity Today*, April 11, 1969, p. 10.

Comments Harold Horton, a British tongues advocate, recognizing the opposition:

"Then there is the notion abroad that tongues are a kind of gibberish, incoherent and nonintelligible, a series of uninterpretable glossal noises. No, tongues were and are languages. They are mostly unknown to the hearers and always to the speakers. But they might on occasion be known to the hearers, as at Pentecost, where the tongues were unknown as they were spoken and known as they were heard."—*The Gifts of the Spirit* (Bedfordshire, England: Redemption Tidings Bookroom, 1946), pages 159, 160.

In other words, glossolalists are thought to speak the

language of the Holy Spirit; the language of heaven; or, as the charismatics like to express it, "the language of angels—the language used by the Holy Spirit for communication with God." Imagine! A holy language of such complicated nature that the human mind cannot grasp its syntax, grammar or meaning; furthermore a language granted only to those who are worthy of receiving it. Being a spiritual language of the high celestial beings, it is thought to be international—in fact, *intergalactic*, and therefore able to cross all known (and unknown) boundaries.

It is no wonder that the charismatics feel closer to God when using their unknown tongue. The very idea of being a confidant of the Holy Spirit, having the chance to speak a language heretofore reserved exclusively for the Spirit to communicate with God and the angels, is sufficient to put most people into a spiritual "high" of unfathomable dimensions compared to which the hard drugs are only mild sedatives.

What is ignored here by both charismatic scholars and enthusiasts is that the human questions regarding the unusual and confusing structure of the tongues remain unanswered.

Most Pentecostals and charismatics, when asked to describe their "tongue," term it "beautiful" and "exquisite." To them it is not only an emotional experience but also an aesthetic one. It is difficult to find criteria for judging an experience so subjective and personal.

This "beautiful" and "exquisite" tongue has become the subject of numerous investigations by prominent linguists, psychologists, psychiatrists, and sociologists;

and even though their professional approach usually differs, the overwhelming consensus of opinion is that the sounds that reach us via the charismatics are not intelligent languages at all—not even in the weakest sense of the word.

After comparing many different voice samples recorded under controlled conditions while tongues speakers were consciously exhibiting their "gift of the spirit," Eugene Nida, renowned linguist of the American Bible Society, says concerning one specific recording:

"The types of inventory and distribution would indicate clearly that this recording bears little resemblance to any actual language, which has ever been treated by linguists. . . . If, then, it is not a human language, what is it? One can only say that it is a form of 'ecstatic speech.' . . . On the basis of what I have learned about this type of phenomenon of 'tongues' in other parts of the world, apparently there is the same tendency to employ one's own inventory of sounds, in nonsense combinations, but with simulated 'foreign' features. At least in West Africa and Latin America, the types of glossolalia employed seemed to fit into this description."—Cited by V. R. Edman, Chancellor of Wheaton College in "Divine or Devilish?" *Christian Herald*, May, 1964, p. 16.

William Welmens, professor of African languages at the University of California at Los Angeles speaks out even more frankly:

"And I must report without reservation that my sample does *not* sound like a language structurally. There can be no more than two contrasting vowel sounds, and a most peculiarly restricted set of consonant sounds; these combine into a very few syllable clusters which recur many times in various orders. The consonants and vowels do not all sound like English [the person's native language], but the intonation patterns are so completely American English that the total effect is a bit ludicrous."—William Welmens, Letter to the Editor, *Christianity Today*, Nov. 8, 1963, pp. 19, 20.

Among linguists, few men are so eminently qualified to evaluate glossolalia as William Samarin, professor of anthropology and linguistics at the University of Toronto. After extensive research in this field for the first comprehensive study of speaking in tongues, he has presented a linguistic analysis that is unequaled in its thoroughness. After comparing all phases of the phenomenon, he reports:

"There is no mystery about glossolalia. Tape-recorded samples are easy to obtain and to analyze. They always turn out to be the same thing: strings of syllables, made up of sounds taken from among all those that the speaker knows, put together more or less haphazardly but which nevertheless emerge as word-like and sentence-like units because of realistic, language-like rhythm and melody. Glossolalia is indeed like language in some ways, but this is only because the speaker [unconsciously] wants it to be like language. Yet in spite of superficial similarities, glossolalia is fundamentally not language. All specimens of glossolalia that have ever been studied have produced no features that would even suggest that they reflect some kind of communicative system."—*Tongues of Men and Angels* (New York, N.Y.: The Macmillan Company), page 227.

He also maintains that he has ascertained that

glossolalia has no grammar because it is a phenomenon, operating without a set of rules which would enable another person to "learn" the "language." What's more—and here he is in agreement with other scholars—he says that on careful analysis "these transcriptions will always expose the linguistic deviant nature of a glossolalist's discourse, notwithstanding the charismatist's claim that glossolalia is neither repetitious nor meaningless banality."—*Ibid.*, p. 78. Significant is his comment on the fact that a person's own linguistic background influences the sounds he utters while speaking the "language of the Holy Spirit."

"What is interesting about these similarities as far as linguists and other social scientists are concerned," he says, "is the all-pervasive influence of one's linguistic knowledge. A human being simply cannot avoid being influenced by the patterns of language once he has acquired its use."—*Ibid.*, p. 121.

One who examines the sounds produced by the charismatics soon discovers that every tongues speaker emits a sound distinctly different from those of his fellow believers—but to them this is nothing unusual. It has been observed that a catalyst is needed for one to burst forth in these supernatural sounds. Linguists have been able to trace certain "tongues" used by several different groups to one and the same "teacher," for it is an accepted procedure for glossolalists to adopt the language used by their spiritual mentor. This, of course, clashes with their publicly announced position that whatever they speak, as long as it is spoken by a glossolalist "filled with the spirit," it is the language of the Holy Spirit that is heard—not a human imitation.

But, you may ask, how about glossolalists living in different countries? By asking that question you have indeed put your finger on a weak spot in their defense, for the "language" produced by a Russian charismatic, for example, sounds entirely different from that emanating from the mouth of a Latin American. The same differences exist between other nationalities. The charismatic tongue of a Chinese bears no relationship to that of the Indian; the Norwegian's is again different from that produced by a Dutch glossolalist. In fact, every language area in the world is supposed to have a legitimate "spiritual" right to manifest its own specific brand of glossolalia—and no matter how they vary from one to another, they are all presumed to be the same language. Mind you, not various expressions of the same language, but the very same language spoken by the Holy Spirit through human organs of speech.

It is at this point that another set of problems arises.

Are we really to believe—inasmuch as there are more than 3,000 known languages in the world, and every language has, according to the glossolalists, a right to its own particular glossolalic tongue—that all of these are nevertheless the same "language of the Holy Spirit"?

I, for one, have never been able to believe that in a heaven ruled by an orderly God, there exists a necessity for the Third Person of the Godhead to address Himself to the other two Persons of the Godhead in what may be three thousand distinctly different languages. I am not willing to believe that this type of confusion is a godly procedure.

Some Pentecostalists and charismatics hold the position that no one can know all of the three thousand languages in use today and that a rule which seems valid for one group of languages does not necessarily apply to another group. To this, William E. Welmens is opposed.

"We do know something about representative languages of every known language family in the world," Welmens writes in his letter to *Christianity Today*. "I am by no means unique among descriptive linguists in having had direct, personal contact with well over a hundred languages representing a majority of the world's language families, and in having studied descriptions of languages of virtually every reported type. If a glossolalist were speaking in any of the thousand languages of Africa, there is about a 90 percent chance that I would know it in a minute."

Robert Glenn Gromacki, Th.D., makes an interesting observation regarding the difference between languages and ecstatic utterances. He writes in *The Modern Tongues Movement:*

"Paul designated the gift of tongues as *gene glosson*, translated as 'kinds of tongues' (1 Corinthians 12:10) and 'diversities of tongues' (1 Corinthians 12:28). This term *genos* refers to a family offspring, race, nation, kind, sort, and class in New Testament usage. It always depicts that which is related to each other. There are many 'kinds' of fish (Matthew 13:47), but they are all fish. There are several 'kinds' of demons in the world (Matthew 17:21), but they are all still demons. There are many 'kinds' of voices (1 Corinthians 14:10), but they are all voices. From this it can be concluded that there are many 'kinds' of languages, but they are all languages. There are several families of languages in the world— Semitic, Slavic, Latin, et cetera. These are all related in that they have a definite vocabulary and grammatical construction. Paul could not have possibly combined known foreign languages with unknown ecstatic utterances under the same classification. They simply are not related to each other."—*Ibid.*, p. 62.

The allegation that tongues are indeed languages—regardless of contrasting expert opinion—has reverberated up into the highest echelons in the land. As a result, the Federal Government financed a scientific study into these claims and uncovered not only pertinent information but also indications of noteworthy side effects.

The research project, initiated in 1965 at the Lutheran Medical Center in Brooklyn, New York, by Drs. John P. Kildahl and Paul A. Qualben, reached some significant conclusions. One finding is that tongues speakers tend to be more submissive, more suggestive, and more dependent in the presence of "authority figures." They also concluded that it was not necessarily the speaking in tongues that made them feel "better" than those around them, but that it was the submission to the authority of the leader in the prayer group that brought about the desired state of euphoria.

William Samarin, who assisted in the inquiry, related in *Christianity Today*, Nov. 24, 1967, p. 39, that where certain prominent tongues speakers had visited, entire groups of glossolalists would speak in his style of speech. Regarding this, the report continues, "So again, the leader was important not only in inducement of the experience, but also in the way in which it was carried out."

In the opinion of the researchers—and again we glean our information from this report—the ability to yield ego in the presence of the one with authority is indispensable to speaking in tongues. Of the accompanying "gift" of interpretation, the report said:

"There was no similarity in the interpretation of the various 'interpreters.' One interpreter said the tongues speaker was praying for the health of his children; another interpreter would report the same speech to be an expression of gratitude to God for a recently successful church fund-raising effort. The most common interpretations were general statements that the speaker was thanking and praising God for many blessings."

Questions anyone?

Much of the material mentioned above is known to many charismatics—but ignored. To them a personal contact with the "Holy Ghost" shrinks all evidence against their gift to insignificance. The real meaning of the work of the true Spirit to "lead men into all truth" has been toned down by the tongues speakers; for them it becomes the spectacular circuslike phenomenon of the tongues speakers. To them, a personal contact with "something" unseen, resulting in an uncontrollable manifestation vaguely reminiscent of the events of Pentecost, is superior to a prayer contact with the everlasting God of the universe, the "Spirit of Truth."

Through organizations such as the Full Gospel Business Men's Fellowship International, the Blessed Trinity Society, and the many Protestant and Catholic charismatic groups the advances of the "Holy Spirit" on the minds of humanity are widely heralded. The approach or method by which the Spirit is introduced to the uncommitted churchgoers does not appear to be as important as the ultimate results, and because of this, many of the nation's top tongues advocates openly advise the use of proven methods to "guarantee" a direct voice contact with the "Holy Spirit."

Dutch Reformed minister Harold Bredesen, chairman of the board of the Blessed Trinity Society and one of the most outspoken leaders in the tongues movement, suggested guidelines to the students at Yale University. He told them "(1) to think visually and concretely, rather than abstractly: for example to try to visualize Jesus as a person; (2) consciously to yield their voices and organs of speech to the Holy Spirit; (3) to repeat certain elementary sounds which he told them, such as 'bah-bah-bah' or something similar. He then laid his hands on the head of each seeker, prayed for him, and the seeker did actually speak in tongues."—Cited by Stanley D. Walters, "Speaking in Tongues," *Youth in Action*, May, 1964, p. 11.

Was it effective? Not everyone really thinks so.

"Of the students involved, some later became unsure that the outbreak was a genuine work of the Spirit. I talked to one who had spoken in tongues when Mr. Bredesen first visited the campus, could do so later whenever he wished, and on his own initiative did so in my presence, yet doubted that it was a work of the Spirit. A devout Christian, he was genuinely perplexed." —*Ibid.*, p. 10. I cannot help but think of the early Mormon example, when Joseph Smith told his followers, "Arise upon your feet, speak or make some sound, continue to make sounds of some kind, and the Lord will make a tongue or language out of it."

Christensen, a Lutheran minister and tongues speaker advised:

"In order to speak in tongues, you have to quit praying in English. You simply lapse into silence and resolve to speak not a syllable of any language you have ever learned. Your thoughts are focused on Christ, and then you simply lift up your voice and speak out confidently, in the faith that the Lord will take the sound you give him and shape it into a language. You take no thought of what you are saying. As far as you are concerned, it is just a series of sounds. The first sounds will sound strange and unnatural to your ear, and they may be halting and inarticulate (have you ever heard a baby learning to talk?)."—Cited by John Miles, "Tongues," *Voice*, XLIV, February, 1965, p. 6.

So here is the prescription, and a simple one at that. To receive the Holy Ghost, the charismatics say, just empty your mind and think of Jesus; focus your thoughts on Christ. Next, while in a mental void, begin to utter sounds, perhaps "strange and unnatural to your ear"; but be confident, they say, for "this is the beginning of your speaking the language of heaven." Another prayer instruction urges its participants to repeat the same meaningless words over and over again until after approximately ten or more minutes the suppliant starts to stumble over his words. "Talk faster than you normally would," they exhort. "This will help you to reach the stage where the Holy Spirit takes over."

In relation to these activities, Raymond Frame, a former missionary, warns:

"Evil spirits can easily find opportunity to operate in the believer's emotional life—especially when the believer is persuaded to suspend all intellectual activity and to yield his will over to an invisible intelligence [whom the Christian, of course, is persuaded to regard as being the Holy Spirit Himself]. For this reason the child of God who becomes preoccupied with that least of all gifts, tongues, places himself in a particularly vulnerable position in relation to the danger of demon depression, obsession, or actual possession."—"Something Unusual," *His*, December, 1963, p. 26.

Every Christian should carefully consider this possibility. God will never force His way into a human life, but Satan, seeing a void mind, eagerly begging for a manifestation of the supernatural, will gladly move in and create within him a counterfeit experience, reputedly to be caused by the Holy Spirit. Considering that he was able to deceive one third of the angelic host during the war in heaven (Revelation 12:7-12), would it be presumptuous to think that he might direct the same tempting power to those who are eagerly reaching beyond Christ for a "shortcut" to salvation?

To what extent a number of tongues speakers will go to make themselves available to the influx of the "Holy Spirit" is quoted by Samarin (*op. cit.*, p. 54):

"Keeping one's hands lifted seems to be (or to have been) one of the traditional Pentecostal practices. Several of my respondents refer to instructions about how one was to hold his mouth and breathe."

J. E. Styles may have been the propagator of this form of inducement. He writes:

" 'Recently I have discovered, through observation of a number of people, that those people who will open their mouths up wide will break forth speaking with tongues more clearly and easily than those who do not. Opening the mouth and breathing in constitutes a step of faith that God will honor.' "

Others claim still different experiences while pleading for the Spirit.

It has been reported that Cho Yonggi, a converted Buddhist and presently a minister in Seoul, Korea, tells the following story in connection with his prayer for divine intervention:

"I saw the Lord . . . and I said to Him, 'Yes, Jesus, I will preach your gospel.' I tried to touch His feet. As soon as I touched His clothes, what seemed to be a thousand volts of electricity flowed into me, and I began to shake. Then strange words came to my mouth, and I began to speak in other tongues."—Quoted by Gromacki, *op. cit.*, p. 40.

Let us compare glossolalia as practiced today with the original Pentecostal experience, and see if the two harmonize. Let us first enumerate the basic facts as found in the story of the outpouring of the Holy Spirit at Pentecost.

1. The apostles were in Jerusalem.
2. They were waiting for Jesus to fulfill His promise.
3. They were all with one accord in one place.
4. They heard a sound as of a mighty rushing wind.
5. It filled all the house.
6. They were sitting when it occurred.
7. The Holy Ghost filled them.
8. Cloven tongues as of fire descended upon them.
9. They received the ability to speak with other tongues.

In this first example of the outpouring of the Holy Spirit found in the New Testament, there is no indication that the disciples (a) prayed fervently to get the

Holy Spirit; (b) prayed for one another to receive the Holy Spirit; (c) laid hands upon one another at that time to receive the Holy Spirit; (d) were assembled to witness to one another with tongues; (e) went through spiritual practice sessions to prepare themselves for the reception of the Holy Spirit.

In the second example, Acts 10:44-46, the Holy Ghost fell on Peter's listeners while he was still preaching, and they began to speak in tongues. Again, no desperate prayers, no disconnected syllables, no laying on of hands, no practice sessions.

The third example is again different, for Acts 19:2-6 shows us that the Holy Ghost was received after true repentance and baptism, and for the first time the laying on of hands, manifesting itself in the ability to speak with tongues. But here, too, we have no indication that they either prayed for themselves or that Paul prayed for them to receive gifts of the Holy Spirit.

Again the question, why do the Pentecostals and the charismatics use the Pentecostal experience of the disciples as their prime example? If their reception of the Holy Spirit is to equal this all-important outpouring, then why are essential elements missing? For the charismatics' experience is not that of Pentecost; nor does it run parallel to Acts 10:44-46 or Acts 19:2-6.

So we must conclude that the charismatics' claim that their gift of tongues is the genuine New Testament experience is erroneous. That their ability to speak untranslatable sounds is real—this fact goes unchallenged. The linguists testify to that. But that this should be placed on a high spiritual level and be the result of the workings of the Holy Spirit has no Biblical support.

We do not question anyone's sincerity; we just question the source.

Spurious tongues, therefore, are not Biblical; they are not godly; they are not from the Holy Spirit. This does not imply, however, that somewhere, today, God may not see the need to supply some of His people with foreign language ability in order to allow them to bring the gospel into a heretofore spiritually dark area. This always remains God's prerogative.

Being a socio-religious phenomenon, glossolalia has aroused the interest of many social scientists; and, being quite outspoken, many of them have made no attempt to conceal their feelings or conclusions.

George B. Cutten, often criticized for his blunt views, maintains that "whatever may be predicted of the psychological conditions of speaking in tongues in the New Testament, it is evident that the experience since then may be classified as ecstasy or allied phenomena. In ecstasy there is a condition of emotional exaltation, in which the one who experiences it is more or less oblivious to the external world, and loses to some extent his self-consciousness and his power of rational thought and self-control."—From "Speaking in Tongues," *Princeton Seminary Bulletin*, 1965.

Dr. Samarin's research has provided him with the conviction that anyone can acquire glossolalia. According to him it is simply for the asking: "The only necessary, and perhaps sufficient requirement for becoming a glossolalist seems to be a profound desire on the part of an individual for a new or better religious experience."—From "Glossolalia as Learned Behavior," *Canadian Journal of Theology*, 1969.

7—C.O.T.S.

Throughout all the opinions advanced by scholars, one common thought pervades, that of attributing the strange tongues to an emotional disturbance, usually excluding the probability of an outside supernatural catalyst. Says Robert R. Gustafson, "In fact, the phenomenon called tongues today appears to provide not only a psychic release from emotional disturbances, but it also appears to provide an emotional high by which one is able to escape momentarily from inward problems and conflicts."—*Authors of Confusion* (Tampa, Florida: Grace Publishing Company, 1971), page 80.

Attributing this disturbance to religious emotionalism, others express it in more ecclesiastical tones. Dr. Stolee makes this observation: "When an unstable or eccentric person, in his search for light or for power, hears of some mysterious experiences of this man or that, he almost invariably hopes that such strange things also may happen to him. His heart is set on this; his prayers center on it. The beatific 'visions,' the 'being in the Spirit' that others claim as their lot he must have at whatever cost. He can and will not take refuge in the plain promises of Christ, but must have some external sign of some inward ecstasy as proof of the 'spirit baptism.'

"If, then, he knows no rivers of living waters flowing out from his life, if no thrill grips him, if no token appears, he is disappointed even unto despair. He envelops spirit fever. All because the mysterious 'baptism' on which he had set his heart is missing."— Stolee, *op. cit.*, p. 81.

If you have ever witnessed a committed charismatic

in action, then you have no difficulty in accepting Dr. Stolee's argument. Once set on receiving the Holy Spirit, the aspirant tongues speaker will stop at nothing to reach the desired state of spiritual bliss.

Studying and comparing examples of tongues and the descriptions of those who uttered them at the very peak of their ecstatic experience have supplied me with sufficient indications that one can speak of a super-emotional state during which the subject appears to be out of touch with his surroundings. Dr. Goodman has observed the same behavior: "The glossolalist does indeed behave differently from ordinary language speakers. . . . We may now suggest that glossolalia be defined as an event of vocalization while the speaker is in a state of disassociation termed TRANCE."—From "Phonetic Analysis of Glossolalia in Four Cultural Settings," *Journal for the Scientific Study of Religion,* 1969.

Many religious reasons have been given for the sudden growth of the charismatic movement, but with atomic regularity many researchers keep coming back to emotional instability as being one of the most dominant factors. Perhaps they have a case, for our society is not half as sane as it used to be. Dr. Gordon B. Hamilton, a Washington, D.C., psychiatrist, concurs. "In the past decade, and particularly in the past five years," he judges, "the general level of sanity has gone down. Conversely, cases of inferiority complex, melancholia, neurasthenia, and psychoneurosis have increased sharply."—Quoted by H. J. Stolee in *Speaking in Tongues,* page 77.

By saying this, Dr. Hamilton touched upon a sensitive

area. It has long been known to researchers that mental instability is indeed one of the recognized avenues to the Pentecostal experience. There is little doubt in their minds that the charismatic movement is just as much psychological as it is spiritual.

Several leading scholars have researched glossolalia from the psychological aspect, and John P. Kildahl writes about the conclusions of one such study: "Tongues speakers have had a profound experience of feeling that they are well; for most of them it has been a physical, emotional, and intellectual experience. Tongues speaking gave them a physical sensation that they had never had before—their tongue did things that seemed impossible. Emotionally, the experience was one of fantastic release, comparable in intensity to sexual orgasm, or to the sense of freedom just after an intense stomach cramp subsides. . . .

"It is easy to understand why tongues speakers are less depressed than nontongues speakers," he continues. "Depression is a feeling that the cupboard of the world is bare, that good things are not possible for oneself, and that the supply of good things in the world 'out there' is terribly limited. A glossolalist believes that God Almighty, Creator of the ends of the universe, is with him and approves of him, and that helping fellow believers surround him and confirm him in his belief that he is all right. It is hard to conceive of a more powerful antidote to feeling depressed. . . .

"Whereas depression is characterized by the feeling of inner emptiness, the glossolalist is filled by the Spirit. Should he feel a bit down, he can begin to speak in tongues and recall that God is with him, that glossolalia is a special gift from God, and that he can unload his problems through releasing his feelings in tongues speech. Each time he speaks in tongues, he performs a physical act which he surrounds with a set of beliefs reconfirming that he is a special person, specially blessed."—*The Psychology of Speaking in Tongues* (New York: Harper & Row, 1972), pages 46, 47.

It has also been said that when speaking in tongues the subjects enter a "pathological condition which is a perversion of the God-intended function of the brain. It is toying with this delicate precision instrument with which God has gifted us. It is transforming the seat of rationality into an irrational machine. In doing so," Donald W. Burdick comments thoughtfully, "a person contravenes God's purpose for man as a rational being." —*Tongues—To Speak or Not to Speak* (Chicago: Moody Bible Institute, 1969), pages 84, 85.

At this point, we must become very selective. While many social scientists blame mental aberrations alone for a person's interest in Pentecostalism—and it has to be admitted that in a number of instances there is a connection—speaking in tongues is not always the result of a sick state of mind. Yet, here too the researchers hold contrasting views. The verbal barrage of discon-nected vocal sounds, emitted under great duress, is— irrespective of what triggers the phenomenon—made up of sounds stored in the subject's mind; and according to psychiatrist Stuart Bergsma, there is a close relationship between this and cybernetics, the basic storage system on which modern computers operate.

Looking at the phenomenon with a clinical eye, Bergsma writes: "Obviously nothing can come out of each individual brain that was not once previously stored there. Material stored may be altered, fragmented, confused, distorted, but cannot be humanly created. Also it is obvious that language . . . which comes out as language in glossolalia, must have been introduced somehow in that person's life. Even if that person was not conscious that he or she had heard those words or that a memory engram was being recorded, these had nevertheless been recorded there. This will explain the very few cases of modern glossolalia [intelligent foreign languages, ed.] , if there are any."—"Speaking With Tongues," *Torch and Trumpet*, November, 1964, p. 10.

His first conclusion is valid. The very fact that Pentecostalists in various countries use intonations and inflections common to their native tongue in their glossolalical discourse, enabling the impartial parties to identify a tongue's national origin, more than proves his point. They take the sounds that have been stored in their brains and reproduce them in a disconnected fashion while "in the spirit." However, it is his position that foreign languages must also have been introduced sometimes in a person's mind before they can emerge as real glossolalia. This view puts him in contrast with the Biblical interpretation of the gift of tongues. The Bible states that in New Testament times these were given as a manifestation of the Holy Spirit—not an occurrence of human recall. Bergsma ignores the possibility of supernatural intervention in the mind of men and denies the existence or even the likelihood of God-inspired utterings.

The ecstatic tongues were judged correctly by Dr. Abraham Kuyper, the late Dutch theologian, long before they had ever become a social status symbol. Said he: "This [the tongues] is not due to man's thinking but in consequence of an entirely different operation. That this is possible we see, first, in delirious persons who say things outside of their own personal thinking; second, in the insane, whose incoherent talk has no sense; third, in persons possessed, whose vocal organs are used by demons. . . . Hence it must be concluded . . . that the use of these [vocal] organs may be appropriated by a spirit who has overcome them."

And this is exactly the direction I believe our findings should lead us!

There is a deceptiveness in glossolalia that is subtle, religiously oriented, and capable of infecting those who are desperate in their search for new light. This sense of desperation is precisely the spark which can explode the human psyche and hurl the seekers into an experience which they think is similar to the one that accompanied the New Testament outpouring of the Holy Spirit. Being surrounded by others who claim the same emotional upheaval, their sincerity and reasoning goes unchallenged; yet this is in itself no proof of the Biblical validity of what has overcome him. It is the sincere devotion to an "all inclusive faith" that has trapped him into a counterfeit manifestation; an experience which does not measure up to the Biblical standards governing the gifts of the Spirit.

5

The Bible speaks of the existence of an invisible adversary, a devil, who is determined to destroy the human race with superhuman power. That this same cosmic being was also the first one ever to introduce a spark of evil in the heavenly courts is also a matter of inspired record.

But there is more to it.

Christians also accept as factual the Biblical concept that the resulting agonizing encounter between the forces of good and evil is to last until the final days of mankind.

It is precisely this intergalactic war that has necessitated the introduction of inspired prophets on the world scene, to act as relay points for the stream of heavenly communications directed to earth-bound sinners. For it is here, on this earth, that the final battle between the two opposing powers will be fought; and it is here that it will reach its climax.

And all the universe will watch it.

One of the greatest prophets of all time, John the Revelator, was especially entrusted by Jesus with a disclosure of the greatest prophecies affecting mankind. While a prisoner of the Roman Empire on the island of

Patmos, he became immersed in scenes of glory surpassing the wildest fantasy. Symbolic prophecies describing threatening judgments were beamed at John, and frightening and severe are Jesus' revelations of the momentous events to take place under the opening of the seventh seal. Under this seal, seven angels are entrusted with specific tasks, and when the sixth angel (Revelation 16:12) pours out his vial upon the great river Euphrates, it happens!

"And I saw three unclean spirits like frogs come out of the mouth of the dragon, and out of the mouth of the beast, and out of the mouth of the false prophet," John solemnly relayed. "For they are the spirits of devils, working miracles, which go forth unto the kings of the earth and of the whole world, to gather them to the battle of that great day of God Almighty." Revelation 16:13, 14.

In his commentary *The Prophecies of Daniel and the Revelation,* Uriah Smith regards these spirits as manifestations of spiritualist power, working their deceptive miracles through the three great religious divisions of mankind, paganism, Roman Catholicism, and apostate Protestantism.

"The agencies which Heaven designs to employ in the accomplishments of certain ends," says Smith, "go through a process of preliminary preparation for the part which they are to enact.

"Thus, before the spirits can have such absolute authority over the race as to gather them to battle against the King of kings and Lord of lords, they must first win their way among the nations of the earth, and cause their teaching to be received as of divine authority, and their word as law.

"This work they are now doing, and when they shall have once gained full influence over the nations in question, what fitter instrument could be employed to gather them to so rash and hopeless an enterprise?"—*The Prophecies of Daniel and the Revelation* (Nashville, Tenn.: Southern Publishing Association), pages 698, 699.

Since the beginning of the modern reintroduction of spirit power in the 1840's in Hydesville, New York, a new unwholesome influence has rekindled the dying flames of paganism and superstition throughout the world.

One of the movement's own leaders admits *why* this is so.

"Shall we come down to the plain simple truth, that the phenomenal aspects of modern spiritualism reproduce all the essential principles of the magic, witchcraft and sorcery of the past?" he questions. "The same powers are involved . . . the same intelligences operating."—J. J. Morse, *Practical Occultism*, 1888.

Perhaps it was still early, but spirit power was indeed moving in, preparing itself for its leading role in fusing the major religious powers on earth in the closing days of history.

Knowing that devil power is the real power behind spiritualism, and that this same satanic force is the influence behind sorcery, witchcraft, and magic, we may well speak of a new era when satanic power will seek to combine paganism, Catholicism, and apostate Protestantism, creating a triumvirate where outright satanic power works side by side and in complete harmony with the three other religious groups—all attired with the cloak of Christian piety.

Not everything accomplished today with the aid of spirit power is officially recognized or admitted as being the result of such supernatural influence. Scientific names have been attached to pure spiritualistic projects in a masterful attempt to make them socially and religiously acceptable. What one medium calls parapsychology, another renames psychicology; yet their aims are identical, for researchers in the field of spiritualism's supernatural phenomena are engaged in attempting to construct a scientifically acceptable basis for a belief in a continuous existence of life after death, whether in a "spirit sphere," or in the "fifth dimension."

"Parapsychology . . . brings hope for world peace, hope for more brotherly relations among men, hope for a new unity of religious faith," emphasizes Dr. Alson J. Smith. "Doctrine, dogma, and form of organization all become secondary to the witness and the power of the inner, supersensory life. Parapsychology will help unify Christendom by emphasizing that supernormal element that all denominations have in common and minimizing those divisive elements that have their root in time obsession."—*Religion and the New Psychology*, 1951, pages 151-174.

Even Sir Arthur Conan Doyle, the grand old man behind the Sherlock Holmes mystery novels and himself a spiritualist of renown, was convinced of this. "The ultimate merit of the revelation, which came in so humble a shape," he said, referring to the birth of modern spiritualism in Hydesville, N.Y., "will be the simplification of religion, the breaking down of the barriers between the sects, and a universal creed which will combine the ethics of real Christianity with direct spiritual communication."—*Beware Familiar Spirits,* 1938, page 83. "Spiritualism, will sweep the world," another spokesman asserted, "and make it a better place to live. When it rules over all the world, it will banish the blood of Christ. Spiritualism has a mighty mission to fulfill, and spiritualists are missionaries of this new teaching of the so-called 'Christ-Spirit.' "—*The Teachings and Phenomena of Spiritualism,* page 72.

Gordon Collier tells of a spiritual entity calling itself the "Master Hilarion."

"This master who [allegedly] fostered the movement of spiritualism over a hundred years ago . . . gave this frank statement of purpose:

" 'My purpose has been, for many years now, to bring to the minds of men through the religion of spiritualism, a greater knowledge of immortality; to prove, chiefly through psychic phenomena, the existence of other worlds around you; to prove that those who have stepped out of their physical bodies and live on in the spirit realms can return to prove the immortality of the soul. . . .

" 'My major concern,' he went on, 'has been to prove that your immediate family lives on after the transition called death. Bringing spiritualism into reality has been my goal.' "—Gordon Collier, *Make Your Own World* (Robert Collier Publications, 1960), page 126.

That these budding activities of the spirit world do not go unnoticed, even by those who do not study the Bible, becomes rather obvious when one looks at the pronouncements on the state of world affairs made as far back as the eventful years surrounding the first world war.

Sir Edward Grey, former British foreign secretary, spoke fearfully of the workings of a strange and mysterious power in world affairs. Said he in 1911, in an address to the House of Commons: "It is really as if in the atmosphere of the world there were some mischievous influence at work, which troubles and excites every part of it."—London *Times*, Nov. 28, 1911.

Another British statesman used even stronger language twelve years later, attempting to identify the deceptive force: "It would seem as if they were all bewitched, or laboring under some doom imposed upon them by devils," Ramsey MacDonald, former British prime minister, admitted in 1923. "People were beginning to feel that there was something devilish in the operations now going on to increase armies, navies, and air forces."—Quoted in "Disarmament Labour Party's Motion," London *Times*, July 24, 1923.

Ellen G. White, prolific writer and religious leader of the turn of the century, also had much to say about the treacherous influences of spirit power on the affairs of men and the combination of religious groupings to be formed under its power at the "time of the end."

"The Protestants of the United States will be foremost in stretching their hands across the gulf to grasp the hand of spiritualism; they will reach over the abyss to clasp hands with the Roman power. . . .

"As spiritualism more closely imitates the nominal Christianity of the day, it has greater power to deceive and ensnare. Satan himself is converted, after the modern order of things. He will appear in the character of an angel of light. Through the agency of spiritualism, miracles will be wrought, the sick will be healed, and many undeniable wonders will be performed. And as the spirits will profess faith in the Bible, and manifest respect for the institutions of the church, their work will be accepted as manifestations of divine power."—*The Great Controversy*, page 588.

Richard Cardinal Cushing, in a pastoral letter, March 6, 1960, backed this idea of religious unity. "For the past several centuries," he wrote, "there has been either a great silence or a species of embittered argument between us and those who, like us, bear the Christian name. Whether in silence or recrimination, there has been a great gulf between us. This gulf we set ourselves to bridge."

This development caused Methodist Bishop James K. Matthews, president of the Massachusetts Council of Churches, to comment: "There is now an increasingly clear voice being heard across what might have been termed an abyss of separation . . . the cry 'Brother'; and that is a cry that has been directed from both sides, and we find that abyss perhaps isn't as broad or as deep as was supposed."

Even Pope John XXIII, regarded as one of the most liberal Catholic leaders of this century, pleaded, "May we hope with a father's love for your return. Honesty demands that we let our separated brethren know that this is our ultimate reason for participating in the ecumenical movement, and that we manifest it in practice by seeking to convert even devout Protestants."

It is Ellen G. White's statement, however, that "Protestants . . . will be foremost in stretching their hands . . . to clasp the hand of spiritualism," that causes the greatest concern; for it is within this smoldering alliance of these religious powers that today's supernatural phenomena will find a home.

It was the late Arthur Ford, ordained clergyman and internationally known Spiritualist medium, who became the single most important agent to advance the fulfillment of this prophecy. It began quite innocently; yet from the moment of its inception, the Spiritual Frontiers Fellowship, brainchild of Arthur Ford, confirmed the validity of Ellen White's vision. Formed in 1956, principally by three men—Albin Bro, missionary and educator; Paul Higgins, a Methodist pastor; and Arthur Ford—it advocated the "encouragement of study of psychic phenomena within the churches as related to personal immortality, spiritual healing, and prayer."

"When we explore the psychic faculties, we are not dabbling in something new and strange," commented Arthur Ford at the group's spring conference in 1958. "We are just trying to remind the people in the churches of something that has always been part of the Christian gospel, but has been neglected for centuries." Comprising more than half of its executive council of twenty-four members are clergymen of the Presbyterian, Methodist, Congregationalist, Episcopalian, Baptist, and other churches; but, in its principles, the organization is merely a front for the promulgation of spiritualist doctrines.

So popular was the medium Arthur Ford among Protestant and Catholic clergy that at one of his seven o'clock breakfast meetings in Greenwood, South Carolina, it was reported that no less than 174 men had turned out to hear him speak on the connection between psychic phenomena and religion. It is highly significant that within the Bible Belt stronghold, every local Protestant minister and Roman Catholic priest was present at the breakfast.

The modern climax of exploring the possibility of human survival after death seemed to have been reached with the formation of the Spiritual Frontiers Fellowship. Some have aptly termed it, the "psychic knock at the church's doors"; but Arthur Ford died, and since then the influence of his organization has greatly diminished. To some it may have appeared as if the initial stages of fulfillment regarding the three unclean spirits of Revelation 16 was being held back, but viewed from a cosmic distance, the process of realization of the prophecy continued uninterruptedly. Even *before* Ford's death, supernatural steps had been taken to assure its continuation. No sooner did the Spiritual Frontiers Fellowship eclipse, did a new face of the supernatural, the gift of tongues, move in, setting the world churches on fire with a revival. So enticing and so influential, it has already been called the greatest spiritual development since the early apostolic church.

That the Protestant and Catholic church leaders had long felt the need for a "unifying force" is by now a matter of public record. Rare is the theologian today who is against this basic idea.

Dr. Albert Outler, one of the foremost Methodist theologians, joined in with many of his colleagues when he said: "This [charismatic movement] isn't my bag. . . . But I think I know some of the gifts and fruits of the Spirit when I see them, and I am convinced that much of what I have seen is for real and just may be a portent of something very much more. . . . It just might be that these odd-ball Catholics with their evangelical concerns for conversion, with their charismatic baptisms and tongues, and with their courageous commitments to reform in both church and society may turn out to have been the vanguards in the third great awakening this country has seen."—Quoted in *New Covenant,* September, 1971, p. 17.

This opinion was practically a spiritual echo of the feelings that captivated other scholars, as is shown when placed side by side with their comments.

Erwin Prange, a Lutheran minister and tongues enthusiast, wrote in *Voice:* "I have been having dialogues with Catholics and with Pentecostals, and it has been a wonderful blessing. In Brooklyn we have two dialogue groups now composed of Lutheran ministers of all flavors and young Roman Catholic priests. We meet and study the Scriptures together, pray together, talk about community problems, and discuss mutual involvement of our parishes.

"Recently I attended a Roman Catholic, Episcopalian, and Lutheran retreat. The Holy Spirit is moving in the Roman Catholic Church. I am convinced that the basic meaning of the charismatic renewal is the reunion of the churches. Not a reunion of compromise, or the creation of the Super-church, but a renovation as to what the unity of the Spirit means."—"A New Ministry," *Voice,* April, 1965, p. 7.

As recently as December, 1972, I had a chance to sit down and talk with Dr. Charles Conn, president of Lee College of the Church of God in Cleveland, Tennessee.

An oldtime Pentecostal minister, Dr. Conn had reached the same conclusion as the more recent converts to Pentecostalism. "The outpouring of the Holy Spirit," he said, "is similar to what was happening at Pentecost. It is genuine. Today it has grown and has gained a place of influence in this generation. It is growing and spreading and is bringing about a spiritual union. I have met and discussed these matters with certain dignitaries of the Roman Catholic Church, I have had them in my services. . . . I have been to the Vatican and have discussed them there. . . . I have discussed them with the Episcopalians, the Lutherans; and there is a unity that is growing! It is a spiritual unity of churches, not an organizational unity. I don't think a total unification of the churches is in the making at this time. But there is a feeling of a spiritual unity that will begin to spread to all the mainline churches.

"One church leader talked to me some time ago and said, 'In the early days we regarded the Pentecostal people as crackpots, and we shut our eyes and hoped they would go away. But when we opened our eyes again, you not only had not gone away, but you had grown so large that we could no longer ignore you. Will you come and take us by the hand and show us the way?'

"The charismatic movement will not cease. This is only the beginning. It will grow until at the time of the Lord's coming it will be very widespread."

You know, I might just as well have quoted the comments made to me while I talked about this with Father O'Connor of Notre Dame University. He is one of the seven Roman Catholic scholars who, as a committee of seven, regulate the Catholic involvement in the charismatic movement.

"Where is all this leading to, you wonder?" he asked, repeating my question. "There is a very good chance that this will lead to a spiritual unification of all churches. I think the renewal of the churches is the main thing, not the tongues. That is just one of the signs. I think the real thing is that the Holy Spirit is renewing the church, and I believe that this will bring them all together in complete unity.

"The gift of tongues as we know it may well be one of the signs of the end and of the coming of Jesus." (This conviction is shared by Bishop Joseph McKinney of Grand Rapids, the chairman of the committee of seven.)

It is highly significant that so many leading theologians of the popular churches support the gift of tongues. But—and somehow this seems almost more weighty—foremost psychics, mediums, astrologers, and parapsychologists interviewed endorsed it as a pure and godly phenomenon.

Looking at the stamp of approval given this phenomenon by these occult practitioners, we have to bear in mind that all of them are engaged in following practices strictly condemned in the Bible. God was not at all secretive when it came to voicing His disapproval of those involved in these pagan rituals.

"There shalt not be found among you any one . . . that useth divination [fortune-telling], or an observer of times [astrologer], or an enchanter [magician], or a witch, or a consulter with familiar spirits [a medium possessed with a spirit or a guide], or a wizard [clairvoyant or psychic], or a necromancer [medium who consults the dead]. For all that do these things are an abomination unto the Lord." Deuteronomy 18:9-12.

The very fact that this text is found among the earliest Bible manuscripts shows that God warned His people of these manifestations at an early time in their history. He condemned them because of the satanic nature of their work. He hasn't changed since that time, and His condemnation still embraces the astrologers, psychics, mediums, and those other prognosticators who work with ungodly principles.

But this does not dim the enthusiasm of today's fortune-tellers.

The South is home to one of the great astrologers of the United States. Known to his thousands of starry-eyed followers as "Doc" Andersen, he operates out of a shack-like office along the highway in Rossville, Georgia; but this unpretentious outward appearance bears no relationship to his status in the area of the supernatural.

Agreeing to an interview about the tongues manifestations, "Doc" observed that he is convinced the tongues are "definitely supernatural." "These people go into this state and speak without knowing how or why," he pointed out, "and I believe most certainly that this is godly. It is most certainly not ungodly! The gift of tongues? I don't believe it can be evil. You bet your life! I believe it's all good!"

When I pressed for a conclusive answer as to the power behind the strange utterances, he retorted, "They are vibrations directly from God. I don't believe it is evil. You hear a lot of people talking about being possessed, but I don't believe that people can be possessed. A person can be evil but not possessed. Talking in tongues is definitely the Holy Spirit moving in."

And evaluating the worldwide tongues movement from his ornately gilded armchair, he concluded, "Tongues are good for people because they are bringing all faiths closer together, and whatever brings people closer together has to be godly!"

A representative of the psychic research faction of the community of supernatural enthusiasts, Hugh Lynn Cacey, was also more than willing to add his views on the subject. Son of the late famed psychic Edgar Cacey, Hugh Lynn heads a psychic research foundation to study his father's supernatural legacy. Reached in his Virginia Beach home, he volunteered: "I have taped the phenomenon for years and have researched it from the psychic angles, and it has several different possibilities. The first possibility, of course, is pure hysteria, where religious people think themselves into a state of hysteria. But there is also the possibility of it being godly, or of an entity possessing someone; a case where the individual functions as a medium for an unknown entity.

"Then there is also the possibility that this is a kind of speeded-up mystical experience vocalized, and it becomes a higher form of communication with God or whatever you call it. . . .

"At this point you ask of course the question, 'Does it do anything to people? Does it make them better people, or does it just produce confusion or bewilderment?'

"There is, however, definite evidence that it is psychic; and by this I mean that it may be a retroactive kind of thing, a sort of primitive memory bank. . . .

"Some organizations like the Spiritual Frontiers Fellowship," he continued, "have endeavored to bring psychic phenomena into the Christian churches. I seriously consider the possibility that the gift of tongues is one of those spirit manifestations that is being brought into the church in general. It will be instrumental in bringing unity to a divided church!"

For fear of being repetitious, I will eliminate most of the other psychic witnesses interviewed. But David Bubar will have to be included, as his views are typical, not only of the clairvoyant mediums, but also of that new breed of psychicologists, the psychic researchers whose aim it is to bring the academic field of psychic research into the nation's classrooms.

Relaxing in his Memphis home, David sorted out his thoughts on the subject, finally vocalizing them into the tape recorder. "I ask, would not the speaking in tongues be a case of tapping into a high spiritual dimension where this language is spoken?" he thought aloud while trying to sort out the various options open to him. "And is it perhaps that this happening is triggered by a 'high' spiritual experience?

"I don't want to go as far as calling it hysteria, but it is close to it. Their 'high' experience brings them in tune with the intelligences of other dimensions.

"Since their experience is an 'electrical happening' to start with, it allows them to slip right into another dimension. It might very well be a holy dimension, for all I know. I can't discern that. Those who have 'linked up' claim to be better because of it—not worse." And then he added seriously, "I don't have to speak in tongues, because I always live in this spiritual high. To me, the idea of speaking in tongues is simply tapping into knowledge that has been stored in other dimensions. But—and this I want to emphasize—we attract only that which we are!"

Trying to explain his non-involvement in tongues speaking, he continued, "I don't talk to Satan. I have no contact with him at all. I only talk to God; and because of my positive attitude I doubt that I am even tempted by Satan. . . .

"Can spirit power really operate the gift of tongues, you ask? Yes, it is undoubtedly spirit power; but I am convinced that it is Holy Spirit power. It is not a depraved thing. You simply cannot get down on a low level where the untrained spirits work and come away with something that is high and spiritual.

"Not having had the experience personally," he concluded, "I don't want to be guilty of calling today's manifestation a counterfeit. If you want to say, however, that the tongues speakers are receiving their ability to speak from their direct contact with beings in other dimensions, then you are undoubtedly correct."

While I was still working on the book, *Jeane Dixon: My Life and Prophecies*, Mrs. Dixon told me repeatedly that there will come a time when all major religions will unify under one God, and that all doctrinal differences will fade away because of this new-found "one-ness" in the spirit. In 1973, while being interviewed on a national television show, she emphasized the same point again, but added to this prediction that there will be a small group of people who will refuse to go along with this unification, but these, she is reported to have commented, "will have to be dealt with."

Having researched the subject extensively before my scheduled interviews with the psychics and mediums, I was not at all surprised by their reaction. All—without exception—approve of the tongues and name God as the supernatural source. They are unified in their conviction that through this new communications medium a common ground needed for the unification of all churches has finally been found. In the ecstatic tongues both Catholics and Protestants have found their common denominator, operated by the same spiritual source whose power they assume to be godly.

In a letter signed "Ralph & Bobbi," a young married couple who attended one of the first modern outpourings of the spirit, at the now famous Duquesne Weekend in 1967, looked back on that memorable event after six years of "spirit fever." One of the paragraphs of their testimony shows the influence it had on their relationship to members of other, non-Catholic, churches.

"Most of our Friday evenings we go to a prayer meeting with Anglicans, Presbyterians, Methodists, Lutherans, and Pentecostals," they wrote. "And for three hours all denominational differences are annihilated, without compromising an inch of our Roman Catholicism. . . .

"Never have we heard the Church of Rome prayed for with such fervor," they concluded proudly, *"as we have at prayer meeting. And with such love."*—*"New Covenant"* (the monthly magazine of the Catholic Charismatic Renewal), February, 1973.

Henry Carlson of the FGBMFI, after having attended charismatic meetings throughout Europe as part of a special European thrust of his group, comments: "I've been in this fellowship ever since it started. First it was mostly composed of Pentecostals. Then some Baptists and Presbyterians began coming in, followed by the Methodists, Lutherans, and others. They all began to get filled with the Holy Spirit, and we thought surely the rapture had come. Then the Episcopalians came in, and we thought maybe it was the end of the world.

"Now the Catholics are worshipping with us. Surely this has to be of God."—*Voice*, October, 1972, pp. 32, 33.

This prompts us to ask the question, How Catholic is this movement?

It has surprised many a religious observer to see the rapidity with which neo-Pentecostalism has been accepted as a valid experience within the Catholic Church by both laymen and theologians alike. Why? The answers vary slightly depending on who gives them. All of these Catholic spokesmen, however, regard the charismatic movement as a Catholic development.

Says Killiam McDonnell: "Within Catholicism, Pentecostalism has met with considerably less resistance than it has within the historic Protestant churches, partly because the concept of the 'wondrous' is more at home in Catholicism than in mainstream Protestantism."—*Catholic Pentecostalism*, page 31.

Adds Father Edward D. O'Connor of Notre Dame: "Catholics who have accepted Pentecostal spirituality have found it to be fully in harmony with their traditional faith and life. They experience it not as borrowing from an alien people, but as a natural development of their own."—*The Pentecostal Movement in the Catholic Church*, page 28. "The spiritual experience of those who have been touched by the grace of the

Holy Spirit in the Pentecostal movement is in profound harmony with the classical spiritual theology of the church."—*Ibid.*, p. 191.

Comments another Pentecostal publication: "That the Holy Spirit would descend on believers in the last times is something that Pentecostal Christians already knew because we have experienced it. But that this blessed promise with the demonstrative phenomenon of glossolalia would reach the Roman Catholics is something which has left us perplexed and surprised."—*The Australian Evangel*, March, 1971, p. 13.

It may have surprised many a Protestant observer, but it surely came as no surprise to the Catholics. To them it appears to be a reemphasis of their basic beliefs, and as such it is rapidly being accepted within the church. "It is not an alien doctrine; it is a Catholic doctrine," they claim, "and as such it is holy!"

That this attitude can lead to extremes became obvious to a *Newsweek* reporter who attended the 1973 Notre Dame University Charismatic Convention. Writing about his experiences in the June 25, 1973, issue he said: "At Notre Dame, a charismatic woman from New Kensington, Pa., complained that her husband, a barber, had refused to attend any more prayer meetings because they made him cry.

" 'He doesn't realize,' the woman theologized, 'that you can have the gift of tears.' And yet another enthusiast praised the Lord for helping her overcome her revulsion for people with acne.

" 'I just didn't understand,' she explained, 'that you could have the gift of pimples.' "

Excesses like these are not commonplace, but do

occur. More in line with the work is the eradication of the doctrinal differences between members of different denominations. A newfound oneness in the spirit is permeating through the spiritual life of hundreds of thousands of well-meaning Christians.

But this claim to be "one" and to be led by the Spirit of truth does not lead the charismatic Catholic to abandon his prayers for the dead or his belief in an eternally burning hell—concepts which are totally unacceptable to some other Christians. This same spirit does not tell him to stop using the saints as intermediaries. It does not show him that for forgiveness of sins one must reach out to Christ—not through a priest.

Does his "Spirit of Truth" tell him to stop believing in the infallability of the pope or in a flaming purgatory? No! He is not told to abandon his faith in these Catholic traditional doctrines; rather he is encouraged by his "brothers-in-the-Spirit," the charismatic Protestants, to retain these beliefs.

The charismatic Protestants, on the other hand, also stick firmly to their individual doctrines. To them LOVE has become the supreme test of faith. They are not unified by trust in God and His guiding principles—they are unified by one common spiritual orgasm! Doctrines are now held to be essential elements signifying a church's individual heritage. And this oneness in the spirit is the spiritual cord that binds them together.

Much has been written by Christian writers about the unconventional doctrines that are to infiltrate Christianity during the closing days of human survival. And they invariably use Biblical prophecy as the basis for this position. Gazing through the prophetic window which allowed her access to tomorrow's tomorrow, the author of *The Great Controversy* wrote:

"The line of distinction between professed Christians and the ungodly is now hardly distinguishable. Church members love what the world loves and are ready to join with them, and Satan determines to unite them in one body and thus strengthen his cause by sweeping all into the ranks of spiritualism. . . . [Roman Catholics], who boast of miracles as a certain sign of the true church, will be readily deceived by this wonder-working power; and Protestants, having cast away the shield of truth, will also be deluded. . . . [Catholics], Protestants, and worldlings alike will accept the form of godliness without the power, and they will see in this union a grand movement for the conversion of the world and the ushering in of the long-expected millennium.

"Through spiritualism Satan appears as the benefactor of the race, healing the diseases of the people, and professing to present a new and more exalted system of religious faith; but at the same time he works as a destroyer."—Ellen G. White, *The Great Controversy*, page 588.

"While it [spiritualism] formerly denounced Christ and the Bible," she continued, "it now professes to accept *both*. . . . Love is dwelt upon as the chief attribute of God, but it is degraded to weak sentimentalism, making little distinction between good and evil. God's justice, His denunciations of sin, the requirements of His Holy Law, are all kept out of sight. The people are taught to regard the Decalogue as a dead letter."—*The Great Controversy*, page 558.

Examining the tongues and their role in today's

Christianity conscientiously and realistically, one realizes the sanction or even quiet acceptance of the phenomenon has become an impossibility. No matter how much the charismatics want to prove the validity of the sounds, accumulated evidence shows that their zealous efforts to give the utterings unreserved Biblical support fall short. The tongues speakers have grossly overstated their case, and in doing so have supplied their opponents with just the right ammunition to destroy their often unfounded claims.

The ecstatic splurts of disconnected vowels, weird and irrational to me, melodious and beautiful to the charismatics, have been termed "linguistic nonsense," "spirit-guided grunts," "untranslatable gibberish," and even less flattering names by the experts who have examined them in the light of the latest available information. No matter the objections of the movement, there seems to be a relationship between the increase in tongues speakers and the growing degree of mental instability. And what's more, both theologians and psychiatrists agree that what is happening now seems to be only the beginning of something much bigger!

Yet, if this were all, the glossolalists' case would still not be hopeless, for statistics in themselves are never absolute proof—only an indication of something. But careful scrutiny of the manifestations as found in the books of Acts and Corinthians fails to provide hope for a Biblical foundation. The misuse of the gift of tongues against which Paul cautioned in Corinthians has no relationship to today's counterfeit "gift of tongues" which has its origin in paganism, heathen ritual, and outright devil worship, the history of which predates the

Pentecostal outpouring of the Holy Spirit by at least a thousand years!

Realizing the significance of this, the charismatic tongues suddenly take on a new and frightening role. The infallibility of Biblical prophecy demands that in order to arrive at a unity of faiths in the closing days of history, the adversary has to provide a common experience or doctrine that will serve as a spiritual adhesive.

The charismatic movement has now supplied that "adhesive" through its manifestation of tongues.

"I believe the charismatic renewal has spread so rapidly in the church these past six years because it is God's work," editorialized Patty Gallagher, a Catholic charismatic convert recently—willfully ignoring the pagan background of her new experience. "He [God] desires to reveal Himself to His people," she continued, "as He spoke to us during the June conference in prophecy. *'What you see before your eyes is just the beginning!'* "—*New Covenant.*

We are now indeed witnessing the lying falsehoods and deceptive methods of the three unclean spirits of Revelation 16, and the position of the prophetic time clock of eternity is no longer a mystery.

But it is not just our conclusions and judgments based on the aforementioned evidence that have brought us to this point.

Early in 1973 I attended a study conference on the charismatic movement, and throughout the proceedings my awareness that this movement was not just a passing fad gained in conviction.

Speaking of his experiences with students who had become charismatics, a young minister I conversed with enumerated the various phenomena that accompany the tongues. Drawing on his many counseling sessions with an impressive number of glossolalists, he submitted for consideration a list of the accompanying phenomena, every one of which was a revelation in itself.

Those who join the charismatic movement and become spiritually involved in its operation depend, in various degrees of involvement, on the following manifestations:

1. *Prophecy*—their leader or another prominent member of a prayer group or general meeting speaking to them for God in an authoritative way.

Considering, however, that the movement is *not* led by God and acts in contrast to the manifestation of the real gift of tongues, we must assume that the power behind these prophecies is not godly, and must consequently come from another source.

God is a jealous God when it comes to protecting His name, and in cases where mere humans assert to speak in His name without His explicit command, His punishment stands recorded. God warns: "But the prophet which shall presume to speak a word in my name, which I have not commanded him to speak, or that shall speak in the name of other gods, even that prophet shall die." Deuteronomy 18:20.

2. *Clairvoyance*—the supernatural ability to foreknow events.

Today, in the United States, where 10,000 professional astrologers and 140,000 psychic-mediums control the minds of over 40 million people, the phenomenon of clairvoyance—once the sole domain of the spiritualists—is widely accepted.

Deuteronomy 18:9 condemns this practice too. Using the ancient designation of "wizard," God counsels His people to disassociate themselves from those who practice this phenomenon.

3. *Clairaudience*—the psychic ability to hear mysterious voices supplying supernatural revelations. This ability, too, is ungodly, as it is an extension of the power of clairvoyance.

4. *Gift of tongues.* As most of this book deals with this phenomenon, there is no reason to attempt to condense all the previous chapters into one paragraph. We must, however, realize that the name of this phenomenon in its present-day form is a misnomer. Whenever the Bible discusses the gifts of the Spirit, it calls them thus because they are specific abilities granted to us, free of charge, for a designated purpose.

5. *Laying on of hands.* This, to the charismatics, is the ability to "transmit" the power of the Holy Spirit to new converts; a practice often accompanied by a feeling resembling a severe electrical shock.

Even though the "laying on of hands" was practiced in the New Testament, it does not tell us that an electrical discharge was the sign of transmission of the power of the Holy Spirit.

6. *Healing*—the ability to perform healing of the sick.

Russel S. Waldorf identifies this "special healing power" for us. Says he, "The energy or vital curative force supplied by a healer is received by him in his capacity as a medium, relayed to him by those doctors in the spirit world who continue their work in their chosen profession."—*Spiritual Healing*, A Centennial Book, page 204.

Another publication gives the following definition of spiritual healing: "It is the sense of this convention that spiritual healing is a gift possessed by certain spiritualist mediums, and that this gift is exercised by and through the direction and influence of excarnate spiritual beings for the relief, cure, and healing of both mental and physical diseases of mankind."—Adopted by the National Spiritualist Association, Rochester, New York, 1909. *Spiritualist Manual,* page 116.

LeRoy Edwin Froom, a careful Bible scholar, after studying both genuine healing and spirit healing, concludes: "There is a fundamental difference between Biblical 'divine healing' and spirit-induced parapsychological 'spirit healing,' though ofttimes they are unwittingly confused.

"Actually a vast separating gulf exists between genuine faith healing, divinely wrought in answer to prayer in Christ's name, and emotional or functional improvements, or alleviation of symptoms, resulting from psychic healing, hypotherapy, or the 'spirit doctor' healings of civilized and heathen lands.

"Divine healing rests upon submission to the transcendent power and beneficent will of God. Psychic healing is, on the contrary, an avowed exercise of interrelated, inherent finite powers, and the interposition of 'spirit powers.' "

7. *Visions*—the reception of supernatural guidance or specifically desired information while lost in a trancelike state of concentration.

While the Biblical prophets received their godly guidance in visions and dreams, experiencing this state is not in itself a guarantee of its godly origin. Today's psychic mediums all claim the ability to receive visions and assure their followers that most of their ofttimes remarkable predictions are the product of such revelations.

But can we honestly trust these visions?

Remember: these visions are received by fortune-tellers, astrologers, witches, mediums, clairvoyants, psychics, and necromancers—practitioners who have been condemned by God. Only true prophets of God meeting the Biblical requirements as outlined in the Holy Scriptures can claim to receive God's messages via visions and dreams.

It takes more than just wishful thinking to be a channel for godly guidance.

8. *Trance*—the total withdrawal from reality during which state contact is made with the supernatural.

The revealing factor about these eight points is not their number or their order, but their significance in this modern spirit-guided movement.

For they are the "fruits" of the spirit guiding the charismatic movement, and its manifestation of tongues.

They're not new.

They have appeared before.

Just ask the National Spiritualist Association of Churches, and they will gladly tell you where and when. They have nothing to hide. They're proud of it.

For it was in 1914, to be exact, that the National Spiritualist Association of Churches adopted a list of definitions of the manifestations of spirit power.

Paragraph 5 is the one we are interested in—and in all honesty, the charismatics should be interested too.

It reads as follows: "The phenomena of Spiritualism

consist of *Prophecy, Clairvoyance, Clairaudience, Gift of Tongues, Laying on of Hands, Healing, Visions, Trance,* Apports, Levitation, Raps, Automatic and Independent Writings and Paintings, Voice, Materialization, Photography, Psychometry."—*Spiritualist Manual,* page 37.

Sounds familiar, doesn't it? Significant it is that the spiritualists have listed their phenomena in order of importance, and that those manifestations occupying the most important place in their churches are synonymous with those that unify the charismatic movement!

Yet some people still ask the question, "Can the tongues be godly?"

To the committed Christian there is only one possible answer. An emphatic NO is the only responsible reaction. The charismatic movement is clearly a new revelation of spiritualism, this time, however, draped with a superficial cloak of godliness.

The writer Ellen G. White, talking about the deceitfulness of spiritualism, made this comment: "The Lord tells us that if it were possible they would deceive the very elect. The sheep's clothing seems so real, so genuine, that the wolf cannot be discerned only as we go to God's great moral standard and there find that they are transgressors of the law of Jehovah."—*Review and Herald,* Aug. 25, 1885.

It all falls in place now.

The identification of the charismatic movement and its master is no longer a problem.

The spiritualists have identified it for us.

But this still does not mean that we are to condemn honest, searching Christians who in all sincerity have been misguided by the movement.

As far back as 1885 Ellen White pinpoint with great accuracy much of the feeling and false excitement that are now raging throughout the churches. As if specifically looking ahead to the 1970's she cautioned:

"One of Satan's most successful deceptions is to lead men to claim to be sanctified, while at the same time they are living in disobedience to God's commandments. These are described by Jesus as those who will say 'Lord, Lord, have we not prophesied in thy name? and in thy name cast out devils? and in thy name done many wonderful works?' Yes, those who claim to be sanctified have a great deal to say about being saved by the blood of Jesus; but their sanctification is not through the truth as it is in Jesus. While claiming to believe in him, and apparently doing wonderful works in his name, they ignore his Father's law, and serve as agents of the great adversary of souls to carry forward the work which he began in Eden, that of making plausible excuses for not obeying God implicitly. Their work of leading men to dishonor God by ignoring his law will one day be unfolded before them with true results. . . .

"None who have had the light of truth will enter the city of God as commandment breakers. His law lies at the foundation of his government in earth and in heaven. If they have knowingly trampled upon and despised his law on earth, they will not be taken to heaven to do the same work there; there is no change of character when Christ comes. . . .

"Those who make a raid against God's law are warring against God Himself."—*Ibid.*

If God decides to reintroduce the gift of tongues as a missionary tool in the twentieth century, then it will undoubtedly be for a specific reason.

But if and when this happens—and indications are that it may come, inasmuch as the counterfeit has already been introduced—we can rest assured that it will not be in untranslatable sounds. It will be real intelligent foreign languages in order to reach unknown tribes with the beauty of the gospel somewhere at the fringes of civilization—before "civilization" will end it all.

To God nothing is impossible—but what He does has to fulfill a purpose.

He just wouldn't be God if He acted any other way.

There is little doubt in the minds of religious observers and concerned theologians that the effects of the charismatic spirit as manifested in the charismatic movement will certainly grow—that it will spread itself throughout the Christian and non-Christian world. The very fact that over forty distinctly different denominations are involved speaks for its growth within Christianity; but it doesn't stop there. Recent dispatches from the Middle East report of glossolalia cells within the Jewish community, and traces are now also being found among those who have committed themselves to Indian mysticism. During the past year Japanese,

Indonesians, Filipinos—all conservative Christians—have locked horns with the emotional appeal of the movement; and where they hoped to win, they lost. The result has been that the spirit's voice can now be observed caressing the larynges of the Orientals.

We are indeed pausing on the threshold of an uncontrollable emotional high that is as much social as it is sensually motivated; and because of this, Christianity balances on the brink of annihilation.

It looks quite grim—and if it weren't for Christ's protective umbrella extended over His church, the future would certainly seem dark.

The future of Christianity is at stake. The fundamental question is not merely whether the charismatic tongues are evil. The real issue is an identification of the Third Person of the Godhead: His qualities, His function, His role in the plan of salvation, and, what's more, His methods of operation.

The average charismatic who reaches into the family rooms via radio or TV or quietly seeks participation in prayer meetings held in "non-believing" churches is typical of the hundreds of thousands of full-gospel Christians who worship God in strange tongues, sincerely believing that it is the Holy Spirit speaking through them.

This is official doctrine.

No one who speaks in tongues takes issue with this. The Assemblies of God, the Pentecostal group par excellence, has gone on record with the following statement of doctrine, supplying the verbal basis for this belief:

"Resolved, That this Council considers it a serious

disagreement with Fundamentals for any minister among us to teach contrary to our distinctive testimony that the baptism in the Holy Ghost is regularly accomplished by the initial, physical sign of speaking in tongues."—Cited by Carl Brumback, *Suddenly From Heaven* (Springfield, Mo.: Gospel Publishing House, 1961), page 223.

In simple words they claim that the vocalizations that accompany the spirit baptism of so many is the test to show that a person has joined with Christ in a deep spiritual experience. The gift of tongues is the criterion. If you don't speak "it," then at least you must be able to exhibit something supernatural or spectacular to authenticate your holy connection.

Is this a reasonable assertion?

Is it perhaps possible that in the process of taking the real Christ out of Christianity the overzealous reformers have mistakenly substituted the "gifts" for the "fruit"?

The Bible makes a distinction between the "gifts of the spirit" and the "fruit of the spirit." Let's take another look at 1 Corinthians 12.

"Now concerning spiritual gifts, brethren, I would not have you ignorant." Verse 1. "For to one is given by the Spirit the word of wisdom; to another the word of knowledge by the same Spirit; to another faith by the same Spirit; to another the gifts of healing by the same Spirit; to another the working of miracles; to another prophecy; to another discerning of spirits; to another divers kinds of tongues; to another the interpretation of tongues." Verses 8-10. And in verse 28 Paul adds apostles, teachers, helps, and governments to the list of spiritual gifts.

The list of the fruit is decidedly distinct from that

of the gifts and is not as involved.

"But the fruit of the Spirit," it states in Galatians 5:22, 23, "is love, joy, peace, longsuffering, gentleness, goodness, faith, meekness, temperance: against such there is no law."

Now where is the connection?

The Bible indicates that where the Spirit dwells, love will be seen. Romans 5:5. Where true love is made manifest, the fruit of that love will be evident, but not necessarily accompanied by a miraculous manifestation of Holy Spirit power. Whereas the earthly desires of men move only in one direction—that of evil—the godly desires of the Spirit move only in the direction of love. It is significant to note that Paul lists nothing but virtues as fruit of the Spirit. True, no one expects a newborn Christian to exhibit all of the fruit of the Spirit at the moment of his conversion, but when the Holy Spirit begins operating within the life of an individual, the fruit of the Spirit begins to reveal the various virtues on an inclining scale—on a growing edge.

There is a close parallel between what Paul says regarding the fruit in Galatians 5:22, 23 and what he says in 1 Corinthians 13:1-8. Because of this, some commentators hold to the conviction that we actually have one fruit of the spirit divided into these various elements. Joy is a manifestation of love, so is faith, and so is hope. Love is the guiding and unifying principle and is the great collective of those elevating qualities.

The Spirit of God is love, and its manifestations are the fruit of this love. This undoubtedly proves that one must have the Spirit of God within him before the various aspects of the fruit of that spirit can make their appearance. The Holy Spirit's virtues expressed in loving fruit are known; but what may we expect to be the attributes, the outward qualities, of the unholy spirit?

We know much about the devil, and what we know isn't exactly complimentary. Waging the war in heaven ages ago because of his ruthless pride, he was finally cast to the earth with one third of the heavenly angels. See Revelation 12:1-9. As the relentless, hateful aggressor in the battle against Christ he has had ample time to show his colors and characteristics. To alert those living upon this battlefield, the Bible lists the identification marks of this spirit of hate, called "the works of the flesh." Galatians 5:19, 20 names these most unlovely traits, including such things as adultery and witchcraft. And why not? The author of this system is himself most unlovely. He (the devil) is a sinner (1 John 3:8); a murderer (John 8:44); a liar (John 8:44); a deceiver (Revelation 12:9); a tempter (Matthew 4:7); the adversary (1 Peter 5:8); and he has the power of death (Hebrews 2:14). These markings are the manifestations of hate, not love.

Because his characteristics differ so radically from those of Christ's Spirit, it should come as no surprise when we realize that the fruit produced in those affected by these attributes will be the opposite to the qualities produced by the workings of the Holy Spirit.

In a previous chapter, I listed part of definition 5 of the group of spiritualist phenomena as adopted by the Nationalist Spiritualist Association of Churches in 1914. Now let's complete the definition.

"The phenomena of Spiritualism," it reads, "consist of Prophecy, Clairvoyance, Clairaudience, Gift of

Tongues, Laying on of Hands, Healing, Visions, Trance, Apports, Levitation, Raps, Automatic and Independent Writings and Paintings, Voice, Materialization, Photography, Psychometry, and any other manifestations proving the continuity of life as demonstrated through the Physical and Spiritual senses and faculties of man."— *Spiritualist Manual*, page 37.

Interesting it is that the spiritualists list these manifestations as phenomena, not as gifts—except for the "Gift of tongues," which is the only one listed differently. However, all are listed as various ways used to prove the so-called immortality of the soul. The gift of tongues was nowhere used in the Bible in connection with substantiating the eternal existence of a bodyless entity after death; therefore it cannot be admitted to this group as a realistic gift of God.

It was not God through the gift of tongues but the devil through the serpent who first said, "Ye shall not surely die," (Genesis 3:4), bringing with those few ill-chosen words the fall of the angels down to the realm of man. Says the *National Spiritualist Association Yearbook*, 1961, page 13: "Spiritualism is God's message to mortals, declaring that There Is No Death. That all who have passed on still live. That there is hope in the life beyond for the most sinful."

Clearly the distinguishing marks exhibited by Satan's followers are not gifts; they are the fruit of an unholy association, and in the same way the manifestations of spirit power are not gifts either. They, too, are fruit; for they are the end-result of total submission to the unholy one.

It was only a few months ago that I sat fascinated in

front of a television screen watching and listening to George Otis of Lear Jet fame explain to Demos Shakarian, president of the Full Gospel Business Men's Fellowship International, the events that led to his association with the charismatic movement. It appeared that even though extremely successful in business, George Otis had experienced a growing dissatisfaction with his spiritual self, and as he listened to a radio broadcast in his car early one morning, he became possessed with the idea of finding the Holy Spirit.

His unhappiness finally directed him to a breakfast meeting of the Full Gospel Business Men's Fellowship International.

Called to the front table by Mr. Shakarian, Otis shared his spiritual disaster with the other businessmen; but when he turned to walk back to his chair, Shakarian shot one final question at him.

"Is there anything we can do for you, Mr. Otis?"

George reeled.

"Yes!" he blurted out. "I want the power of the Holy Spirit to come into my life." No sooner had he uttered those words than ready hands were laid on him from all sides, and he began to speak with sounds which had never before passed his lips.

So you wonder— Is there perhaps the wisp of a possibility that this might indeed have been the Holy Spirit moving in? It clearly states in Luke 11:13 that the Holy Spirit will be granted to everyone who will ask for Him. ("How much more shall your heavenly Father give the Holy Spirit to them that ask him?") This is certainly sound Christian doctrine. If we were required to do something special in order to qualify for the reception of the Spirit, then we would have salvation by works. But it is also very plain that someone would not or should not be asking for the Holy Spirit in all its fullness unless he really meant to live in such a manner as a life in Christ would indicate.

In the charismatic's experience, love is supreme. Granted, they call upon the Holy Spirit with the utmost of sincerity; but theirs is basically a doctrine of emotional love, and nothing is to surpass this. Since God is the embodiment of love, one has to assume that this all-consuming Christian love is the manifestation, the expression, of a deep fellowship with God, not merely in words but also in deeds. Discussing the relationship of emotional love to Christian sincerity with a charismatic is much like playing a game of spiritual poker.

The religious writer, Ellen G. White, seriously questioned this relationship in her masterpiece, *The Great Controversy*:

"The sanctification now gaining prominence in the religious world carries with it a spirit of self-exaltation and a disregard for the law of God that mark it as foreign to the religion of the Bible. Its advocates teach that sanctification is an instantaneous work, by which, through faith alone, they attain to perfect holiness. 'Only believe,' they say, 'and the blessing is yours.' No further effort on the part of the receiver is supposed to be required. At the same time they deny the authority of the law of God, urging that they are released from obligation to keep the commandments. But is it possible for men to be holy, in accord with the will and character of God, without coming into harmony with the principles which are an expression of His nature and will, and which show what is well pleasing to Him?"—Page 471.

Her reasoning is fully supported by the Holy Scriptures. "He that hath my commandments, and keepeth them, he it is that loveth me: and he that loveth me shall be loved of my Father, and I will love him, and will manifest myself to him." "If a man love me, he will keep my words: and my Father will love him, and we will come unto him, and make our abode with him. He that loveth me not keepeth not my sayings: and the word which ye hear is not mine, but the Father's which sent me." John 14:21, 23, 24.

Spiritual charades are of no value in the face of such evidence of God's requirements. Love, says Christ, results in willing obedience to all of the God-given commandments. When one does not keep these commandments, it is a sign that love toward God is lacking. One surely doesn't need a superior intellect to realize the meaning of these texts. Proclaiming faith in the experience of love without exhibiting a love for Christ, expressed in the keeping of all his laws, is a useless exercise in emotionalism.

Even though the Holy Spirit will be given to those who ask for Him, the fulfilling of the request is nevertheless dependent on believing in Christ and strictly adhering to His rules of living. See Acts 5:32.

When Christ finally honors this trust and faith in Him with the bestowing of the Holy Spirit, He calls Him the "Spirit of truth." "Howbeit when he, the Spirit of truth, is come, he will guide you into all truth." John 16:13.

Sanctification is a continuous process fanned on by growing in truth. This can never be accomplished without conscientious Bible study (John 17:17); yet, once a glossolalist has received the "spirit," all further development of eternal truths in him is usually terminated. His ability to speak in untranslatable mutterings has convinced him that through this experience he has received Heaven's sanction for his way of life. (After all, he has the Holy Spirit, hasn't he?) He now firmly believes that henceforth additional spiritual light will be a spontaneous act of God, not necessarily the result of his trying to attain a Christlike life through following the dictates of the "Spirit of truth" revealed in the Bible, the word of truth.

He doesn't realize that it is never the spectacular that proves godliness. Look at Christ's life. Even He did not perform a miracle unless it was essential to provide a much needed service to suffering humanity. He set definite boundaries for the use of miracles, and even under the threat of death He could not be coerced to violate His own established rule.

Satan tempted Him in the desert and tried to persuade Him to make bread out of a stone.

Christ's answer?

"It is written, Man shall not live by bread alone, but by every word that proceedeth out of the mouth of God." Matthew 4:4.

Once more He was tempted—this time in the Holy City on the pinnacle of the temple. The devil wanted Him to perform a miracle to prove His divinity and dared Him to throw Himself down.

"Jump, Jesus," he may have said in the colloquial speech of those days. "Jump, and let's see if Your angels will really catch You."

But again Christ refused. This, too, would not be a miracle for the sake of humanity.

The devil tried one more time, offering Christ all the kindgoms of the world in return for one simple prayer to him.

"You can have all this," he slyly coaxed. "Everything will be yours. Just do as I ask."

But Christ had His divinely imposed limits. He owned it all, everything was His; all creation was His—all humanity was His with its faults and diseases. He was the One who had created Lucifer in the very dawn of creation (cf. Colossians 1:16 and Ezekiel 28:11-19)—and now the created wanted Him, the Creator, to kneel to him in blind adoration?

"Then said Jesus unto him, Get thee hence, Satan: for it is written, Thou shalt worship the Lord thy God, and him only shalt thou serve." Matthew 4:10.

When toward the end of Christ's earthly life King Herod asked the Prisoner to perform a miracle before his eyes, Christ refused to speak even a word to him, least of all demonstrate supernatural powers. When He was on the verge of death, His tormenters wanted Him to come down from the cross to prove His divinity; but again He chose not to comply. Christ never involved Himself in the spectacular for the sake of vanity.

The opposite, however, is true of the charismatics of today.

In a recent discussion on the subject, Gary Patterson, pastor of the Collegedale, Tennessee, Seventh-day Adventist Church, enlarged on this.

"As things become less spectacular," he pointed out, "they tend to become more significant. Being overawed with the spectacular is not exactly the way to build a personal relationship with someone. God seeks a personal relationship with His people, and that is what salvation is all about; to restore us to a face-to-face relationship with God.

"It may sometimes be necessary for God to use the supernatural to reach us, but after He has done that, He desires to teach us with His own wisdom. Jesus came to us in a spectacular manner, but He could not in human nature be everywhere at once. Therefore, when He went away, He sent the Holy Spirit, that He might teach us and lead us into all truth.

"The Christian who wishes to stay with the spectacular and never moves on to an understanding will never really know God. The spectacular can be counterfeited, and a mind that never moves on to a higher plane of thinking will be taken in."

It was an insistent ringing of a tireless telephone that awakened me out of a restful slumber. Lazily I reached for the bedside table and took the receiver off the hook.

A dark unfamiliar voice called out to me.

"Mr. Noorbergen? Are you Mr. Noorbergen?" the voice sounded cold, muffled, and typically Irish.

"Yes—that's me. Who is this?"

There was no identification on the other end of the line. He just ignored my question.

"What time do you have?"

I quickly glanced at my watch.

"Ten minutes past three."

"Right! Now listen. A friend is willing to meet you. Be outside your hotel lobby in exactly fifteen minutes from now. We will pick you up—and remember: no recorders, no cameras. Also we know what you look like, so *no* substitutes!"

A dry click in the receiver cut his voice at the end of the last syllable. Again I was alone in my hotel room, but this time I was fully awake with that old familiar sense of excitement hankering for a climax.

It had been a long road to this phone call. It all started when one of my magazines asked me to go to Ireland to get an exclusive interview with one of the top three men of the outlawed Irish Republican Army. In the past I had accompanied one of its teams on a bombing raid to the little Irish border town of Enniskillen; on another occasion I had watched some of the men training in hand-to-hand combat—but the dream of every journalist to meet the man behind the scenes had always remained elusive. However, it all changed after one week in Dublin hunting for the right contact. I found it in the chief public relations man of Aer Lingus, Ireland's national airline.

"I can't tell you how to get to him," he said with a laugh when I casually asked him for some new leads, "but I can give you some names of people you should know." And quickly he jotted down some names and phone numbers.

"I'm still with Army Intelligence reserve," he said, frowning, glancing up from his note pad. "We *know* these people know, but naturally they won't tell us."

It had been in answer to some of my phone calls six days prior that this invitation had finally come through. Each of the names had professed ignorance of anything to do with the illegal IRA, but I nevertheless had asked them to hold on while I read them a list of people they could contact to establish my reliability. I handled six names that way—and then sat down and waited.

Now, in the dead of night, exactly fifteen minutes after the mysterious phone call, I sauntered out of the hotel, quickly blending with the dimly lighted street—a nameless figure waiting for a faceless man.

A cab slowed down in front of the hotel. The door swung open.

"Get in," an urgent voice called out. "We must hurry!" Two groping hands reached for me and pulled me inside while the car picked up speed.

"Mr. Noorbergen?" the "telephone" voice queried.

"Yes, but—"

"Sorry," the voice cut in. "We have to blindfold you and frisk you. You can meet our friend, but you have to come as you are. You will see him when we get there, but he will always remain nameless, faceless, and unidentifiable." Threateningly he continued, "And that goes for all of us. We will find you if you ever break this trust."

It has been a while now since that memorable ride through the dimly lighted suburban streets of Dublin, but somehow I can still recall the thoughts that were racing through my mind while firmly locked in between the two thugs in the back seat.

"I wonder who he really is— Wonder where he lives— What is his real function within the IRA— Wonder what he looks like—" And of course the ultimate question of prime importance to a reporter, "Will I get what I need once I have contacted him?"

Is it any wonder this episode began to play through my mind when I started researching the subject of the Holy Spirit?

Having dug deep into the charismatic movement, I ferreted out the reasons for the sudden popularity of this spirit-guided phenomenon. It became apparent to me that the entrance of the modern tongues has been carefully timed to coincide with the introduction of a new spiritual disease called "emptiness of the soul"; a self-loving condition that exists in a life built around a spiritual vacuum where Christ is but a name, and the Holy Spirit is nothing but a formless wisp of undefined power.

In true prophetic form Ellen G. White foresaw that this new misplaced emphasis would impede God's work, and she repeatedly warned against it. Notice this statement:

"The enemy of souls desires to hinder this work [of religious revival]; and before the time for such a movement shall come, he will endeavor to prevent it by introducing a counterfeit. In those churches which he can bring under his deceptive power he will make it appear that God's special blessing is poured out; there will be manifest what is thought to be great religious interest. Multitudes will exult that God is working marvelously for them, when the work is that of another spirit."—*The Great Controversy*, page 464.

To me, Christianity is realism in the most profound sense of the word. It does not merely stop at saying, "I believe in Christ"; it includes a fusion with all He represented while on earth. It also means that the ability to identify the negative and discern the workings of Satan is in itself not to be the end of something; rather it is to be a stepping-stone to higher spiritual development. Thus, while knowing and warning others against the devil's new manifestations is right and commendable, we are obligated to go one step further. We are cognizant of the areas of human frailty through which Satan works; but is our knowledge of the Holy Spirit also of such magnitude that we know all about Him and know why and how He operates within our lives?

Every good news story answers five major questions, usually in its introductory paragraphs. If the words of Jesus promising *all* of humanity the gift of the Holy Spirit wasn't good news, then my sense of values is all wrong.

It was in a discourse with His disciples that Christ first gave the news of His contingency plan to them.

"And I will pray the Father, and he shall give you another Comforter, that he may abide with you for ever; even the Spirit of truth; whom the world cannot receive, because it seeth him not, neither knoweth him: but ye know him; for he dwelleth with you, and shall be in you. I will not leave you comfortless: I will come to you." John 14:16-18.

But, as in the case with so many items worth remembering, the impression it should have made on them was soon effaced from their memory, buried between the struggle and envy within the ranks of the disciples for power positions and influence in Christ's new kingdom. Not until after His death did the true meaning of it dawn upon them; for the promise was repeated in Christ's parting remarks when He said, "But wait for the promise of the Father, which . . . ye have heard of me. For John truly baptized with water; but ye shall be baptized with the Holy Ghost not many days hence." Then, in answer to their question, He assured them, "Ye shall receive power, after that the Holy Ghost is come upon you." Acts 1:4, 5, 8.

Christ's work on earth was limited in that He could reach only those with whom He came in personal contact. Now, however, through His Comforter, the "Spirit of truth," the entire world suddenly became the recipient of Christ's Spirit, and the cross became the bloodstained door, the only door through which anyone attacked by Satan could find refuge. Escape was promised to everyone by Christ through the Spirit of truth.

It is undoubtedly one of the greatest news stories of all times; equal in significance to the event announced by the angels over the fields of Ephrata, just outside the sleepy town of Bethlehem, a mere thirty-three years before.

If it is a news story, where are the five major points that are to be found? One cannot get through a college journalism course expecting a passing grade without making them a part of his classwork. Known as the "five W's," the "who, what, where, when, and why," they are the hooks on which everything is hung.

Let's apply them to the Holy Spirit and see where it

leads us; for if He is of such great importance that Christ included the announcement of His coming in His parting remarks to His disciples, then we owe it to ourselves to become thoroughly acquainted with this Being.

Let's look at the five W's again.

Who is the Holy Spirit? *Where* is the Holy Spirit? *What* is the Holy Spirit? *When* came the Holy Spirit? *Why* did He come? Aren't they all relevant questions? Wouldn't you want to know the nature of a new friend before meeting him, especially if recommended so highly by none other than Jesus Christ? Wouldn't you want to know where to find him? Wouldn't you want to know something about his history or know when he came the first time so you could check on his performance and see whether he had really lived up to the high expectations people had of him? But above all, wouldn't you really like to know why he had agreed to take Christ's place on earth?

For many years, the Holy Spirit remained an elusive power to me. I had developed, of course, a firm belief in God as my Creator and in Christ as my Redeemer, but the third part of the Trinity, that undefinable something that has the power to convict us of sin and to guide us into all truth has always been the mysterious element in religion.

A growing awareness of the power of the charismatics' spirit led me to inquire into the qualities of the Spirit Christ had sent as His Comforter. It has been said that we will never be able to define or explain clearly the nature of the Holy Spirit because God has not revealed it to us. In fact, John 16:13 states quite plainly that "he shall not speak of himself."

Have you ever tried to find power in a wisp of smoke, to see depth in the dark, or to feel substance in the fragrance of a flower? To many, the Holy Spirit is just as intangible. God hasn't really hidden Him from us. His desire is for us to be on very intimate terms with this third part of the Godhead; and because of this, His revelations about this often mysterious power can be found throughout the Bible. There is no need of uncertainty concerning this Comforter of Christ, but we must rely entirely on revelation to discover His attributes. I, for one, would never be satisfied to try to develop a close personal relationship with an undefinable something, and fortunately, God doesn't require this of us. The Holy Spirit is undeniably distinct from the Father and the Son, yet He possesses the qualities of a person. He is a person, but not in the same sense as we know earthly beings. The Bible never attempts to describe the form of this spiritual Comforter, but it nevertheless ascribes to Him personality traits that cannot be part of a shapeless bolt of Supreme Power. This is part of His inscrutability.

The Bible tells us that He has the ability to *think*, for He has a mind (Romans 8:27); He can be grieved (Ephesians 4:30); He knows the things that God knows (1 Corinthians 2:11). He is a teacher (1 Corinthians 2:13); an intercessor (Romans 8:26); a witness (Romans 8:16); a guide (John 16:13). Other Bible passages describe Him as the Spirit of God; the Spirit of Christ; the Spirit of truth; the Intercessor. We must be extremely careful that we don't think of Him as a flash of power or merely a conscience that tells us when we have erred.

We have all viewed paintings depicting Christ while on earth, and because of this and Genesis 1:26, where God said, "Let us make man in our image, after our likeness," and verse 27, "so God created man in his own image, in the image of God created he him; male and female created he them," we usually think that it is Christ's image involved here. But it is the image of all three beings of the Trinity. We are made in the image of God the Son; we are made in the image of God the Father, but we are also made in the image, the "likeness" of God the Holy Spirit. Just because we call Him Holy Spirit does not make Him any less real. In fact, the angels are called "ministering spirits" (Hebrews 1:14); but that does not necessarily mean that they are not real beings! They are—but of a different order from humans. Using the modern vernacular, we might say they live in a different "dimension."

It is in this invisible dimension that the Holy Spirit works, but the effects of His endeavors are nevertheless real! He is an intelligent, personal being, separate in that He has His own specific function as part of the Trinity. Yet He is unified with the other two Persons of the infinite Godhead ruling the entire universe. In spite of all this, He is humble enough to come down and become the personal representative of a crucified Jesus, so that Christ could appear before His heavenly Father as man's mediator. No matter what happens to the individual beings of the Trinity, it is to this diversity and personal operation that the Trinity owes its greatness. Augustine once said that "the inner relationship of the Holy Spirit and the members of the Trinity is such that both each are in each and all in each and all in all and all are one."

This in actuality is another way of saying that we really don't know how to explain it. We will never be able to take the element of mystery away from the Trinity; if we could, God would no longer be God. There is a unity of the Godhead which could not function without these three beings existing as they do, and we should accept this in faith.

In a recent discussion on this subject with Dr. Thomas H. Blincoe, associate professor of Theology at Andrews University, I caught a glimpse of the greatness of the triune God.

"Trying to explain the three-in-oneness of the Trinity," Blincoe said, relaying his innermost thoughts, "would be like trying to explain all the mysteries surrounding the nature of Christ. In His case there are two natures in one person—only *two,* and we already have problems explaining that. To explain this godly mystery without diminishing either the human or the divine nature of Christ is simply impossible. If we can't explain the union of God and man in one person, then how can we mortals attempt to explain the concept of three divine beings in One? There are infinite mysteries facing us, and let's thank God for that, for without them God wouldn't be God.

"The relationship between Jesus and the Holy Spirit is most sacred and intimate. Even though the Holy Spirit came in Christ's place, we cannot separate His work from that of Christ, for He came to bear witness of Christ, not of Himself. Today we live not in the physical presence of Christ but in the spiritual presence."

I often think of the Holy Spirit as a "spiritual extension" of Christ. Where there were limitations in His "reach" while with us here on earth, now suddenly His loving embrace encompasses everyone everywhere through His spiritual power. Yet, in every instance when we attempt to put a godly principle into human words, the word "extension" is a poor approximation of the real meaning. There are so many "extensions" to Christ that even if this one could be explained, we would immediately find ourselves on the shimmering threshold of more mysteries, with each one introducing us to a new "extension" of Christ.

Reasoned out by Dr. Robert Francis, it works like this: "If God is love," he explains, based on 1 John 4:8, "and God is a Trinity (Matthew 3:16, 17; 28:19, 20; Jude 20, 21), then it follows that this godly love is three; God the Father, the lover; Christ the Son, the beloved; the Holy Spirit, the indispensable divine component of love; for while God is One, God is also Three. A good example is our human relationships. The man and his wife are 'one,' yet we know they are different personalities. But as much as 1+1=1 (wife + husband = a family unit), even so 1+1+1 (God + Christ + the Holy Spirit) still equals one and yet the Trinity.

"Applying this principle to the atonement, we see that the Father is involved in the atonement; the Holy Spirit is involved in the atonement, and so is Christ. Each played His specific part in the divine process, and inasmuch as all three were equally as deeply involved, the role each one played was necessary and indispensable."

Since the resurrection, the omnipresence of Christ with all its holiness is manifested to us through the constant attention of the Holy Spirit, and the Godhead is once again pressing onward to fulfill the promise of redemption. Never again will God the Son be the same as He was before He assumed the role of our Saviour. Says Ellen G. White: "In taking our nature, the Saviour has bound Himself to humanity by a tie that is never to be broken. . . . God gave His only-begotten Son to become one of the human family, forever to retain His human nature."—*The Desire of Ages,* page 25.

The Holy Spirit's relationship to the Father is now somewhat different. He is not just the Holy Spirit, He is now also the Comforter. It appears that through Christ's resurrection, a new phase, a new dimension of the Godhead has come to the surface. The Holy Spirit suddenly takes on a new role and moves to the forefront; to the fluid battleline of the soul. How varied this new task actually is becomes evident when we compare it to His activities prior to Christ's incarnation.

In the dawning days of this world the Spirit was active in the process of creation, according to Genesis 1:2. When the plan of redemption was implemented, the Spirit expanded His executive function (Genesis 6:3), particularly as it related to convicting men of sin.

In Exodus 31:3 still another area of the Holy Spirit's activities was revealed when God declared that His Spirit would be involved in distributing gifts and skills needed for the construction of the tabernacle. When Christ returned to heaven after successfully completing the first phase of His earthly rescue mission, the Holy Spirit became the special representative of God in a manner, a degree, and a dimension that we cannot find in the Old Testament—a function which will continue until the end of time.

It blossomed into a new fullness as far as this earth was concerned.

There was always a unity of purpose in the triune power of the Godhead.

There has always been complete harmony among the three members as to the function each one was to fulfill, yet never before did the compassionate character of the Holy Spirit emerge so clearly as when He assumed His role as Paraclete (Comforter, advocate, or intercessor) on earth.

The Father is still the Source of life; the Son is still the Redeemer; but now the Holy Spirit has joined man as an intercessor and a teacher by virtue of mutual agreement among the members of the Godhead.

A true friend has come to what otherwise would have been known as the "legion of the doomed," and has brought with Him the battle plan of the enemy.

We know now who the Friend is.

When can we expect Him?

Bumper stickers have been known to convey the strangest messages to those drivers who get too close.

I saw one of them recently, and after I had managed to inch nearer to read the words, I wished I hadn't.

This is what it said: "IF I MOVE WITHOUT A DRIVER, IT MEANS HE'S BEEN RAPTURED."

I changed lanes, passed the car, and looked in. Sure enough, the driver was still inside, together with his wife and their little curly-headed son. Putting up his index finger to signal, "With God," he smiled confidently at me, and so did his wife.

I smiled back and let my foot depress the gas pedal just a little bit farther.

I had no doubt that he was sincere in his belief that at any moment Christ would come to whisk them away in "secret rapture" to escape the wrath of the seven plagues. He was sincere—but is that really all it takes?

I also vividly remember a favorite uncle of mine who was brought up as a church-going member of the Dutch Reformed Church but who had decided to stop attending. In fact, once the Calvinistic idea of predestination was explained to him by his church elders, he stopped going to church altogether.

"If God has elected me to be saved from before the foundation of the world," I would hear him say, grinning carelessly, "then I'll make it. He'll see to that. But if not, then I won't stand a chance anyway." And with this as his belief he ventured through the remainder of his life, firmly adhering to his misconception of God's plan of redemption.

He too had faith—but was it the right kind?

Today things aren't much different. A short time ago my seatmate on a 747 jetliner nudged me as we were taking off from the Los Angeles International Airport.

"Are you saved, brother?" he asked, with a solemn look of concentration on his face. "Do you have faith?"

For a moment I was tempted to ask, "Faith in what?" but his sincerity was too obvious, and our flight ended amidst a comparison of Christian ethics.

To be honest, the twentieth-century emphasis on the Holy Spirit is startling. Throughout the earth's history of wars—highlighted by political stalemates called peace—patriarchs, apostles, popes, and reformers have attempted in varying degrees to elevate the human mind—but our dope- and sex-oriented culture of today indicates that in a sense they have failed miserably.

They have failed because even though God reached down, humanity seldom looked up; and as a result, a true connection was never effected.

It was in utter desperation and in everlasting love that the Trinity decided to surpass the cloud of smoke and the column of fire. While the Father looked on in silent admiration, God the Son descended in person, successfully defeating the devil on the battleground of his choice.

And then it happened.

With a rushing as of a mighty wind, the Holy Spirit came to earth, ten days after Christ's ascension into heaven, and rested on the assembled apostles to fulfill the promise of the Saviour.

What is often forgotten today is that the Holy Spirit arrived on His new mission in the year A.D. 31. We don't have to pray Him down; He came to stay and has been here ever since. He is a friend who is constantly reaching out for us.

Paul had a question for the Galatian believers:

"Received ye the Spirit by the works of the law, or by the hearing of faith?" Then he goes on to inquire, "He therefore that ministereth to you the Spirit, . . . doeth he it by the works of the law, or by the hearing of faith?" This informs us that we can indeed make a "spiritual" contact with this Third Person of the Godhead who already resides with us through the "hearing of faith." In Acts 5:32 a condition is added. "And we are his witnesses of these things; and so is also the Holy Ghost, whom God hath given to them that obey him."

It is significant that Paul lists the most passive of all human organs, the ear, as the channel through which the Holy Spirit first makes contact with man. The ear is completely devoid of action, compared to other parts of the body. It does not see; it does not feel; it does not move. It is simply there—waiting patiently. It is nothing but a receptacle for vibrations. But it has one unique quality: It cannot be shut off from within. We can close our eyes, limit our touch, even breathe through our mouth to cancel out our sense of smell; but the ear continues uninterruptedly, sensing sound vibrations that are beamed at it from all directions. It is this inert ability that qualifies the ear to be the channel through which the Holy Spirit first reaches the soul. A fitting example of this is found in the book of Acts where Peter was commanded to visit the home of a Roman centurion to preach the gospel to the people, and "to testify that it is he which was ordained of God to be the Judge of quick and dead." Acts 10:42.

"While Peter yet spake these words, the Holy Ghost fell on all them which heard the word." Verse 44.

This text does not list any exceptions. "All them which heard the word" received the Holy Ghost.

The Spirit does not "sit and wait" in patience and despondency hoping that perhaps today another soul will accept Christ—forcing him into action. That philosophy is contrary to the Bible. Christ went out to seek the lost, and the Holy Spirit works in much the same fashion.

While the Holy Spirit is anxiously waiting for people to ask Him to enter their lives, His reaction does not necessarily depend upon such an invitation. It is perfectly in line with the heavenly ordained task of the Comforter to enter a human life and bring solace and relief from bondage without even being invited. He convicts us of sin, and this does not have to wait for our initiative. The Holy Spirit can veritably come into a human life unrequested, simply through the "hearing of faith." Once the soul has been exposed to His power, an investigative process begins.

I do not believe that He will force His way into a human life. However, often the individual is not consciously asking for the intervention of the Spirit; yet he may be unconsciously seeking assistance to overcome his shortcomings. It is at this point that God moves in. He knows the innermost emotions of a lost soul and activates the curing process by having the Spirit speak to him. This in itself is no guaranteed road to salvation; there is still the free will that governs all our actions. Sensing the small voice of the Spirit, the individual now has a choice either to accept or to reject the counsel. Accepting Him in faith will open the way for an unlimited influence and working of the Spirit.

As man responds, the Spirit will penetrate still deeper into his life, bringing with it even more guidance and understanding, even more love and faith until the convert attains the spiritual condition normally designated with the term "new birth." That is the place where the individual makes a conscious intelligent decision to let Christ take over his life.

"Lord, I can't do it alone," is the common mental plea at this point. "Here's my life. You handle it for me." It is the Spirit who first took the initiative because of man's desperate yearning for help, but it is the individual who now builds on the foundation constructed by the Spirit and erects the superstructure that eventually becomes the temple of God.

And now comes the most beautiful part of all. When the human soul takes over and consciously begins to add to the value of the new being, the Spirit increases His work. The greater man's initiative, the more increased the Spirit's workings become; and on and on, hand in hand, Spirit and man labor unceasingly across the bridge of sanctification that leads to godliness.

Let's remember: Sanctification is always the result of the workings of the Holy Spirit, but man's cooperation is needed. The Spirit cannot bring the grace of God into the life of a passive partner. Without this union of action and reaction, growth in Christ is an impossibility. The true work of the Holy Spirit can never actually be separated from the cooperation of man.

Dr. Douglas Bennett once commented: "No one can really describe exactly how the Holy Spirit functions, but we do know that His activity is very diverse and very vital. I suppose we could try to summarize it by saying that Christ is the source of *eternal* revelation, and the Holy Spirit is the source of *internal* revelation. Christ is the advocate in heaven; the Holy Spirit is the advocate in the soul."

The Holy Spirit endeavors to re-create us in His image; that is, He will put all His power behind His effort to make us holy. This is the most elementary of all teachings about the Holy Spirit. But even though this conforms us to Christ's standards of righteousness, it does not mean that once we become a Christian we lose our individuality. Fanaticism resulting in loss of one's original personality, and piety eventuating in social lethargy and other excesses which make a Christian forsake his drive and initiative, cannot be regarded as the outflow of a life governed by the Holy Spirit. In a life with the Spirit there is never a loss of personality or individuality. What the Holy Spirit really does is to enlighten the person. He guides him and strengthens him. He gives him 20/20 spiritual vision enabling him to see what the work of the Spirit entails and where it leads. The Holy Spirit magnifies the good qualities of the individual and diminishes the degrading character traits. This is what will make heaven so wonderful. Christ is not trying to transform the Christian community into a rubber-stamp society where everyone acts and behaves in unison or where all will sit piously under a fig tree and perform on holy impulse. He wants an army of individuals, everyone dedicated to the same cause, all appreciative of God's great sacrifice, and each one expressing love in his own way. I sometimes experience an uneasy feeling when in the company of those who claim to be true children of God, yet have lost all personality. Personality and intelligence are identifying marks given us by the Creator, and God will never require us to shed these marks that make man great.

In 1905 Ellen G. White gave a clear description of the way in which the Holy Spirit works with human beings. Here is what she said: "The brain nerves which communicate with the entire system are the only medium through which Heaven can communicate to man and affect his inmost life."—*Testimonies*, Vol. 2, p. 347.

Now notice a few seemingly unrelated statements.

"The use of liquor or tobacco destroys the sensitive nerves of the brain, and benumbs the sensibilities."—*Temperance*, page 59. "The man who has formed the habit of using intoxicants is in a desperate situation. His brain is diseased, his will power is weakened. So far as any power in himself is concerned, his appetite is uncontrollable. He cannot be reasoned with or persuaded to deny himself."—*The Ministry of Healing*, page 344. "Reason is paralyzed, the intellect is benumbed, the animal passions are excited, and then follow crimes of the most debasing character."—*Temperance*, pages 23, 24.

Do we realize the significance of these statements? We know from Scripture that the Holy Spirit comes to us by hearing the word of God; making the ear the first element in the process of communicating and transmitting the words of the Holy Ghost to our soul. This is only the first step. The vibrations that touch the eardrum are quite meaningless until they reach the sensitive nerves of the brain where they are then transformed into thought. It is this "thought center" that is the focal point of all spiritual activity. Nothing functions without control centers. For example the United States has several control centers: one in Colorado, governing the Strategic Air Command; one in the Pentagon, controlling the activities of all United States forces; one in the White House, from which the President can direct both military and political activity; and other centers, though inactive at the present, which could direct retaliation at a moment's notice if and when the United States ever comes under enemy attack. In the same way we, too, have our control mechanism that is on a constant alert status—but ours can function correctly only if maintained by the Holy Spirit.

Because of its prime importance, our nerve center has become the scene of a continuous fight between the forces of good and evil. Aware that he must conquer the mind before he can possess the body, Satan devotes most of his attention to devising ways for destroying the sensitivity of the brain.

Is he successful?

Dr. Melvin H. Knisely, professor of anatomy at the Medical University of South Carolina in Charleston, has provided an insight concerning this that speaks for itself.

Reporting on Dr. Knisely's work in *Listen* magazine for December, 1969, Glenn D. Everett writes: "For years it has been known that alcoholics suffer serious brain damage, but most doctors have dismissed this as simply one of the end effects after years of hard drinking, along with liver damage, kidney malfunction, and heart disease often seen in alcoholics at autopsy.

"Dr. Knisely has now demonstrated that this brain damage is not merely an end effect, but occurs progressively from the first cells destroyed by the very first drink a person takes, and that the damage accumulates relentlessly with every drink he takes thereafter at any time or place." Additional research has shown that blood cells tend to stick together as the result of the introduction of small amounts of alcohol into the bloodstream, and this eventually develops into a "sludge." That's where the trouble begins. Neurons, the "thinking" cells of the brain, require a tremendous amount of oxygen for an efficient operation. As the sludge blocks oxygen flow to the neurons, they cease their normal functioning. If the blockage persists for as little as fifteen minutes, the brain cell dies. The late Dr. C. B. Courville commented that alcohol indeed damages every part of the human nervous system. He pointed out that the cerebral cortex, that part of the brain responsible for thinking, is badly damaged by alcohol and that the cerebellum, concerned with the coordination of various muscle groups—voluntary and involuntary—can also suffer serious damage, for nerve cells in both the cerebral cortex and the cerebellum die as a result of alcohol consumption.

What did Ellen White say?

"He [the alcoholic] cannot be reasoned with." "Reason is paralyzed, the intellect is benumbed." Interesting statements, these, which suddenly seem to take on new significance, for science tells us that these indeed do result from the use of alcohol. Other tests show that experimental rats which were fed meals common to many Americans developed an abnormal taste for alcohol when coffee and spices were added to their diet. All this points toward the conclusion that the use of stimulants and narcotics seriously impairs the proper functioning of the neurons and desensitizes the human mind, preventing it from correctly interpreting the stimuli reaching it from external sources.

Does the Holy Spirit enter the mind via the "hearing of faith"? He most certainly does, but how can we expect the human mind to interpret the voice of the Spirit accurately if the mind is damaged by detrimental living habits? How can anyone honestly expect to hear and obey the true voice of the Spirit of God if he consciously continues to lay obstacles in the path of the Holy Spirit?

The Spirit comes into a human life on the hearing of the word of God, but our individual reaction to the voice of this benevolent intruder is dependent upon our readiness to receive Him, which in turn bears a direct relationship to our living habits.

Since the devil is acutely cognizant of the importance of the human mind, is it any wonder that he systematically tries to short-circuit the electrical channels of the brain through dependence on alcohol, narcotics, and other everyday stimulants? He is actually working to block physically the only avenue through which the Spirit of God can reach him.

The one major factor distinguishing us from the animal world is our reasoning power. Created as beings in God's own likeness, we have the ability to reason, to think, to decide matters affecting us and our surroundings. But where the satanic plot to block the mind does not succeed through the introduction of drugs and depressants, numerous other methods are deployed, some subtle, others not so subtle, yet all aimed at the same target—the reasoning powers of the God-endowed mind.

God will never produce an experience by by-passing the human senses while simultaneously introducing more exalted truths into the human life. With Satan, however, things are quite different. He does not operate on an elevated, reasonable level. His tactics are diametrically opposed to what one would expect from an all-loving superhuman being. With trances, clairvoyancy, and mediumship, he has infiltrated minds receptive to his power; and relentlessly he clutches these in a spiritual vice, stimulating their every nerve with supernatural impressions that eventually become so indelible that they corrode the paths of reasoning and keep the mind from receiving the beautiful signals of God.

The manifestation of tongues today, it seems to me, is undoubtedly one of the most flagrant abuses of the use of the human mind. Believing that the Holy Spirit can perform on command, charismatics employ a counterfeit ceremony of laying on of hands or subject themselves to uttering an unending stream of meaningless syllables, resulting in a tongues experience that can hardly be associated with the Holy Spirit. This happening circumvents all reasoning processes and takes total control of the mind, obliterating the individual's ability to distinguish truth from error and injecting into the mind an emotional and physical sensation which consumes all reasoning, and substitutes sensuality for love.

With frightening reality I can still recall the events of World War II. I remember the merciless armies of the occupying power crossing the scantily defended borders, and like a cloud of locusts devouring the beauty of the land for five dreadful years. With torture chambers and concentration camps, the swastika depressed all resistance in an attempt to sever the channels of communication with the outside world.

But what happened?

The resistance grew, and where one partisan died, others quickly took his place, until the "antibodies" of the land had become accustomed to the adversary and found avenues to resist and improvise in order to reestablish the paths of communication with the liberators. In the end, freedom was regained.

But where in warfare the struggle for possession of the body takes precedence over that of the mind, the battles of the spiritual world go just the opposite. With the mind in control of the body—the underlying principle of modern-day brain-washing techniques—all efforts of Satan to conquer the world are concentrated on the human mind. It is there that the battle between the Holy Spirit and the prince of evil is being fought, for he knows that if he can prevent the mind from remaining receptive to the impulses of the Third Person of the Godhead, then his cause will triumph.

The Holy Spirit came with renewed power in A.D.

31. He is still here and calls on us daily. It is this knowledge that keeps Satan active. It is our constant concern for salvation that should be our sign that the Holy Spirit is unceasingly pleading for entry into our life, our mind.

He is here for us to accept; not through an experience of the spectacular, but through the quiet openness of faith that is based on and rests in God's love.

Not long ago, an eminent theologian confronted me after having given careful study to my manuscript for *Glossolalia, Sweet Sounds of Ecstasy.* He was clearly unhappy and troubled and didn't attempt to hide it.

"I have many wonderful friends who are Pentecostals," he exclaimed in a disturbed voice. "They're good Christians; good neighbors. Do you really mean that everyone who believes in Pentecostalism is on the side of evil?"

Not being as well-grounded in the Bible as he is, I recall stumbling around for the right answer. In my heart I knew that many are deceived by this experience and live their Pentecostal belief in the utmost of sincerity. But can an emotional happening resulting from a violation of God's law be termed a "godly experience" even though it is the product of sincerity?

For more than an hour we talked in the privacy of a friend's office. However, on parting, we were nowhere closer to the solution than before. It was not until days later that I found a statement that put the answer in concise form.

A Bible student put the matter in these words: "Pentecostalism does not lead to Christ, but away from Christ. The central theme of the charismatic movement is this: When a believer accepts the Lord Jesus Christ, he is converted and is baptized by water into Christ. But that is not enough. There is something more. The believer must go beyond baptism into Christ. He must enter into a higher subsequent experience called the baptism of the Holy Spirit. In this way, Pentecostalism divides the Trinity. It makes a dichotomy of being baptized into Christ and being baptized into the Holy Spirit. When this premise is accepted, the human mind cannot help but conclude that the Holy Spirit's baptism is superior to the baptism of Jesus Christ, or that the Holy Spirit is beyond Christ and has something better to offer than the Lord Jesus Christ."—Author's personal file.

Obviously the view of the charismatics is anti-christian, and there is nothing in the Bible to substantiate their position.

"But when the Comforter is come, whom I will send unto you from the Father," Christ promised in John 15:26, "even the Spirit of truth, which proceedeth from the Father, he shall testify of me."

"Howbeit when he, the Spirit of truth, is come, he will guide you into all truth; for he shall not speak of himself; but whatsoever he shall hear, that shall he speak; and he will shew you things to come." John 16:13.

These and other texts suggest that the Holy Spirit always ministers in the name of Christ; He always testifies of Christ. The relationship between the two is so intimate that one might conclude that the impartation of the Holy Spirit is the impartation of the life of Christ. They cannot be separated. In sending the Holy Spirit, Christ changed His personal human presence with omnipresence; his limited human power with omnipotence. Throughout the Holy Scriptures we find that Christ is the only mediator between God and man. The very basis of Pentecostalism—that is, denying that Christ is the only one through whom we can go to the Father and that He alone is the mediator between God and man—gives it a decidedly antichristian stamp. Again, as previously mentioned, sincerity alone is not sufficient if it is grounded on the wrong premise.

The Holy Spirit is Christ's representative on earth, but as He is a part of the Trinity, the salvation offered us by Christ would be impossible without the ministry of the Holy Spirit whom He sent as His Comforter and Guide.

The relationship between Christ and the Holy Spirit is extremely close. It will probably never truly be appreciated until the time designated as the latter rain when the Holy Spirit will be manifested to humanity in a greater way than ever before and will show His divine power in unlimited magnificence.

Says the Christian author Ellen White: "Let Christians put away all dissension and give themselves to God for the saving of the lost. Let them ask in faith for the promised blessing, and it will come. The outpouring of the Spirit in the days of the apostles was the 'former rain,' and glorious was the result. But the latter rain will be more abundant. What is the promise to those living in these last days? 'Turn you to the stronghold, ye prisoners of hope: even to day do I declare that I will render double unto thee.' 'Ask ye of the Lord rain in the time of the latter rain; so the Lord shall make bright clouds, and give them showers of rain, to every one grass in the field.' [Zechariah 9:12; 10:1.] "—*Christian Service*, page 251.

In recent years conscientious Christians have been conditioned to see satanic overtones in everything that is unusual. God is not always given sufficient credit for the mysterious things He accomplishes, for the working of the Spirit is not in all instances recognized. Because His actions aren't always accompanied by the spectacular does not mean that He does not work at all. The influence of the Holy Spirit in a human life is recognizable without question; for as a radioactive isotope is traceable while in the bloodstream, so also the sojourn of the Holy Spirit in the soul always leaves a "trail of love." It may not be spectacular, but it is observable. Every spiritual manifestation vibrates constructive discernible overtones. How else can it be, for the creative power of the omnipresent Spirit breathes love, justice, holiness, and truth? He distributes spiritual gifts—all qualities of which He shared with us in order that we may be restored to the image in which God created us in the beginning.

The subject of the Holy Spirit and His role in the plan

of salvation is magnificent yet unfathomable. It is almost understandable therefore, that individuals who do not have a deep enough conviction about the value of Christ to keep His commandments can become overenchanted with the more mysterious aspects of the Spirit's work. For in doing so, they completely lose sight of the reasons why He has come or the real magnitude of expanding His work here on earth.

"His gifts are something special," someone once remarked to me. "They are a revelation of the mysterious aspects of God, and it is by taking in this supernatural aspect of the Godhead that we can become one with Him." What is overlooked is that God never intended for us to become supernatural beings; He merely furnished the supernatural to direct the way to Him. It's a spiritual lamp that will guide us toward the shimmering light at the end of the long dark road.

There is no denying that the more mysterious phases of the Holy Spirit are the most appealing ones, and even the apostle Paul did not discourage the early Christians from desiring to obtain the more spectacular spiritual gifts as first granted the believers at Pentecost.

"Follow after charity," he advises in 1 Corinthians 14:1, "and desire spiritual gifts, but rather that ye may prophesy." Evidently there must have been a reason for Paul to stipulate this course of action. Could it perhaps have been his zeal for spreading the gospel of Christ to the boundaries of the known world? The very meaning of the word "prophecies," Greek *prophēteia* which should be translated "to speak publicly," not necessarily "to make predictions," as is often thought today, seems to indicate that Paul wished for more active speakers. He also knew the critical value of the other spiritual gifts which God had reserved for His people; and throughout the entire chapters 12, 13, and 14 of the first epistle to the Corinthians he delves deeply into a discussion of the importance of the gifts of communication, more so in fact than the other spiritual gifts. The perceptive reader can see why. The Corinthians had placed too much emphasis on spiritual gifts and had developed an abusive attitude toward the communicative gifts of tongues and interpretation. In an attempt to rectify this, Paul enumerated all the known gifts of the Spirit, emphasizing that each one had its own specific place in the Christian life and in the church.

"Now there are diversities of gifts, but the same Spirit. And there are differences of administrations, but the same Lord. And there are diversities of operations, but it is the same God which worketh all in all. But the manifestation of the Spirit is given to every man to profit withal." "But all these worketh that one and the selfsame Spirit, dividing to every man severally as he will." 1 Corinthians 12:4-7, 11.

This certainly leaves no room for disagreement. According to the words of Paul, every Christian is the recipient of at least one gift of the Spirit. The manifestations of the Spirit are accorded to every man, with each one receiving that which the Spirit feels will befit him best because of background, spiritual development, or other reasons known only to the Spirit. It is not up to us to judge the wisdom of the Spirit's actions or His choice of human receptacle for one of His godly gifts. We are not to be law-makers, but law-keepers. He decides who is to fill a certain role, and we are to obey.

Much of today's emphasis on the gifts is because of the un-Biblical position that the gifts of the spirit can be acquired through human endeavor. The very fact that the Bible speaks of the "gifts" of the Holy Spirit indicates that they are given directly by the Spirit without interference from us or without anyone being able to pressure the Holy Spirit into a certain course of action. They can most certainly not be earned: They are under His control, and He gives them as He deems necessary. Charismatics do not subscribe to this view. "I can speak in tongues whenever I feel the need for it," is the assertion often heard. In harmony with the guidelines handed down from convert to convert, they close their eyes, open their mouths in faith, and proceed to utter a stream of unfamiliar syllables claimed to be the language of the Holy Spirit. Aside from the absurdity of it all, the very claim that they can command the Holy Spirit to speak through them in His heavenly language whenever they so desire contradicts the concept of the Holy Spirit's superiority. Compelling Him to perform at the will of a mere human makes the Third Person of the Godhead subservient to man; consequently, of what value is the role of the Holy Spirit or the role of His counterpart in the Trinity, Christ, if man can place himself above God?

The Holy Spirit distributes spiritual gifts as a spiritual extension, a spiritual addition, to the natural gifts with which we were born. Upon becoming a Christian, not only do we have such natural gifts of hearing, sight, and reason, but these are now supplemented by one or more of the spiritual gifts conferred upon us by the Holy Spirit. A violation of the use of these gifts does not necessarily place us in jeopardy of losing this bestowed sense (or senses) but rather increases our responsibility; for now we are not merely transgressing against the use of an inborn gift but we are guilty of deliberately misusing a spiritual treasure entrusted to us by Christ's Comforter.

My little son Randy once placed me in a rather awkward position. He had done something for which he should receive a rather severe punishment; however, since he was only four years old, I debated for a moment what to do in order to impress upon him the seriousness of the offense.

I finally decided on a spanking and told him to come.

Standing before me, he fastened his wide-open eyes on me, and as if searching for a weak spot in my attack, he carefully examined every line on my face.

He stood there looking very thoughtful; then he talked. And once he started, I knew I had already lost the battle.

"I know you're angry, Dad," he blurted out, his little face breaking out into a confident smile, "but you still love me! I am your boy; I am Mommy's boy; but I'm also Jesus' boy!"

And then he climbed up on my knee and kissed me.

And do you know what happened? I just didn't have the heart to spank "Jesus' boy." I'll think twice before doing that! By invoking the love of Jesus he blotted out his offense. It is this same love that keeps us in a constant state of forgiveness, in readiness to receive the gifts of the Spirit of God.

The responsibility of opening ourselves up to be a fitting receptacle for a gift of the Spirit is a grave one.

For even though it is individuals who receive the gifts, they accept them in their function as members of the body of Christ.

Paul says as much in the twelfth chapter of 1 Corinthians, where he compares the church of Christ to the human body and the spiritual gifts of the church to the members of the physical human body.

"For as the body is one, and hath many members, and all the members of that one body, being many, are one body: so also is Christ. For by one Spirit are we all baptized into one body, whether we be Jews or Gentiles, whether we be bond or free; and have been all made to drink into one Spirit. For the body is not one member, but many. If the foot shall say, Because I am not the hand, I am not of the body; is it therefore not of the body? And if the ear shall say, Because I am not the eye, I am not of the body; is it therefore not of the body? If the whole body were an eye, where were the hearing? If the whole were hearing, where were the smelling? But now hath God set the members every one of them in the body, as it hath pleased him. And if they were all one member, where were the body? But now are they many members, yet but one body. And the eye cannot say unto the hand, I have no need of thee: nor again the head to the feet, I have no need of you. Nay, much more those members of the body, which seem to be more feeble, are necessary: and those members of the body, which we think to be less honourable, upon these we bestow more abundant honour; and our uncomely parts have more abundant comeliness. For our comely parts have no need: but God hath tempered the body together, having given more abundant honour to that part which lacked: that there should be no schism in the body; but that the members should have the same care one for another. And whether one member suffer, all the members suffer with it; or one member be honoured, all the members rejoice with it. Now ye are the body of Christ, and members in particular. And God hath set some in the church, first apostles, secondarily prophets, thirdly teachers, after that miracles, then gifts of healing, helps, governments, diversities of tongues." 1 Corinthians 12:12-28. Other texts add more gifts to those listed above which are: faith, wisdom, knowledge, discerning of spirits, interpretation of tongues. Verses 8-10. The gifts of ministry and exhortation are added in Romans 12:3-8, while Ephesians 4:11 also lists evangelists. Totally there are sixteen gifts—and these are only the ones revealed to us.

In relation to Paul's allegory of the members of the physical human body, it seems quite evident that in the same ways that the various members of the body complete the whole man, so the diverse spiritual functions granted the Christians through the gifts of the Holy Spirit are to complement the church, working together within the confines of the church for maximum effect. Even though the gifts are distributed to the different parts of the body of Christ (the members of His church), in reality these gifts belong to the church to be used for its edification and not that of the individual. It is at this point in the Christian experience that the minister is to work closely with the individual members of his congregation; for it is he who is to help the person uncover that particular gift given him by the Spirit. It is practically a foregone conclusion that anyone, upon accepting Christ, receives at least one of the gifts of the Spirit, but we may not always realize this or know immediately in which area of spiritual development this gift may be.

Says Dr. Thomas Blincoe: "As the New Testament unfolds, one can see that while the Holy Spirit has been sent out into the whole world to convince everyone of sin (John 16:8), there is also a more specialized sphere of operation, and that is the church. The individual bears a message to others, but so does the church. Both have to work harmoniously together; and while the Spirit is seeking to develop individuals and remold them into the likeness of Christ, they become more of a homogenous unit with the church. Their witness will become more efficient, more congruent with the message they preach; and a true Christian development through the Spirit will assure them there will be no credibility gap. The testimony of their life will not contradict the testimony of their words. When they preach love, they practice love. When a Christian preaches forgiveness, he has to practice it. The church preaches Christ's principles; but unless its members practice His principles both in words and deeds, our lives become an empty shell and we damage the reputation and hamper the effectiveness of the church.

"The power of the Holy Spirit is not an earth-moving sort of thing, but rather a more subtle type of power. This element of the Spirit is called love, and it moves right in; and once people are caught up in it, they're won over by it, and they end up by expressing and channeling this received love to others through showing them the fruits of that spirit."

Then my theologian friend gave some specific applications of the principles he had discussed. "You know, you might have individuals who move a certain way for a given time, and if this appears to be Godlike, everyone marvels at their sudden change. But if Christ isn't really in it, they won't be able to continue. If on the other hand, the individual's new life is in direct response, in reaction to supreme love, then his behavior toward his friends is a reflection of his newfound relationship to God. Where that is the case, nothing can be done to stop it, for there is nothing stronger than love. In our own experience, love is a powerful all-persuasive influence—and this is only love on a human level. Imagine the unlimited, unselfish power of God's pure love; the universal element after which Christian love is fashioned. It is this type of godly love that He is injecting into the life of the Christian."

Thus, it is not a force enabling the recipient suddenly to perform superhuman feats; nor is it a supernatural influence that will transform spiritually impoverished individuals into instant magicians; nor will it give them ability to do something no one else can do. The power of the Holy Spirit can accomplish miracles—but He normally doesn't work that way. His influence is usually marked by outward expressions of love, manifested in what is known in Christianity as the "fruit of the spirit."

Galatians 5:22-26 lists the results of a Spirit-filled life: "But the fruit of the Spirit is love, joy, peace, longsuffering, gentleness, goodness, faith, meekness, temperance: against such there is no law. And they that are Christ's have crucified the flesh with the affections and lusts. If we live in the Spirit, let us also walk in the

Spirit. Let us not be desirous of vain glory, provoking one another, envying one another."

There is a decided distinction between the "fruit of the Spirit" and the "gifts of the Spirit" even though they are of such nature that they cannot be separated from one another. A full acceptance of Christ results in the appearance of all the fruit of the Spirit in the human life. All may not be apparent at the moment of conversion; but as faith develops and understanding grows, the fruit of the Spirit begins to multiply in the maturing Christian's life. In the converted one the night of confusion and spiritual darkness changes. Honesty, love, devotion, and understanding supplant all the emotional reactions that once gripped him in chains; and joy much deeper than simple pleasure takes over. No longer will love appear as just another product of human matrimony; it will glow with a divine light. The fruit of the Spirit will begin to manifest its various virtues with an inner warmth, a spreading happiness, a love, and a lasting feeling of spiritual well-being. These traits will grow until all are recognizable attributes of the true Christian. This fruit, therefore, is not the same as the gifts; for whereas the fruit of the Spirit is a natural result of a life that has accepted Christ without reservations, the gifts of the Spirit are just that—*gifts*—and only God the Holy Spirit can grant them.

"Follow after charity, and desire spiritual gifts," Paul admonishes in 1 Corinthians 14:1, clearly emphasizing that whereas charity (love) is what the Christian should use as the pattern on which to rebuild his life, spiritual gifts are not something that can be obtained by merely following after those who have them. He counsels the

Corinthians to desire spiritual gifts. Of course, there are moments when one of these gifts may seem necessary, and God does not forbid His children to ask for that which they feel they need; however, it will always remain His prerogative to give or not to give. Only He can decide who is to receive it—that's why He is God.

While I was traveling home from a speaking engagement in the Midwest, I scanned a newspaper and chanced upon an article illustrating the basic misunderstanding of this very principle. Writing about the 20,000 Roman Catholics who had gathered at Notre Dame University in Indiana for their International Conference on the Charismatic Renewal of the Church, Bob Olmstead, correspondent for the Chicago *Sun-Times* reported the following in the paper's June 3, 1973, edition: "At the general prayer sessions, the worshipers are cautioned that the Spirit will be allowed to speak only through those chosen to represent them on the platform. If anyone else approaches a microphone, he will be denied it."

This mocks the power of the Holy Spirit, for no longer do they permit the Spirit to work through whomever He wishes. No! In the modern world of the charismatics, the Holy Spirit will be "allowed to speak" through some, but His action is to be repressed in others, depending upon the decision of the leaders in charge.

The Bible teaches just the contrary.

Concerning the various gifts of the Spirit, Paul says in 1 Corinthians 12:11: "But all these worketh that one and the selfsame Spirit, dividing to every man severally *as he will*." He decides, and inasmuch as He is God, there is very little we His creatures can do to alter His will or command Him to stay away and keep His gifts. The very fact that the exclamation of tongues through the charismatics can be suppressed or commanded to perform indicates that this simply cannot be the Holy Spirit's voice. For God certainly can override our decisions and distribute His gifts wherever He wills.

There is no Bible text that can be used to show that we can either increase or decrease our share of the godly gifts. When the Lord guides us and we accept His authority, He will lead us into a wider ministry for Him; and when He senses our need for additional spiritual gifts, He will bring them into our lives. There is nothing we can do to influence Him one way or another. Only He can and will decide the what, where, and when; for they are all under the direct control of the Holy Spirit.

Let's look at the gifts again and give careful note to the sequence as listed by Paul. Perhaps he is trying to tell us something. This is his order in 1 Corinthians 12:28:

> Apostles
> Prophets
> Teachers
> Miracles
> Healing
> Helps
> Governments (administration)
> Diversities of tongues

Several listings of spiritual gifts appear in the New Testament, but in my opinion this is the only instance where they are ranked in order of importance. This sequence appears logical; and God, being a God of order, would undoubtedly have it no other way. The gifts are all important in their own right, and, when used for the purpose for which they are given, they magnify God.

A careful comparison between the gifts of the Spirit and the fruit of the Spirit illuminates a beautiful contrast between the two godly qualities.

The converted individual begins to experience the manifestations of the fruit of the Spirit from the very moment of accepting Christ. The reception of the gift of helps at this point in time causes these manifestations of love. The virtues of this fruit are set apart from the gifts of the Spirit; they are separate, yet related. The fruit is a natural consequence of a full surrender to God and is so received.

The gifts of the Spirit, on the other hand, do not appear to be as consequential as the fruit, although we may safely assume that when God recognizes the new Christian's ability to "handle" the gift of helps, he may extend to him more specialized gifts if and when needed. But it is the fruit that signifies a true Christian. Not the gifts. A product is never recognized by the tools used to make it. It is its compliance to the manufacturer's exact specifications that makes it recognizable as a quality product.

Is there no way to invoke the power of the Holy Spirit and have Him supply one of His gifts when we feel it necessary?

Ellen White, previously quoted, in a magazine article in 1899 wrote appropriately concerning this. Said she:

"The Lord is more willing to give the Holy Spirit to them that ask Him than parents are to give good gifts to their children. Then ask. Believe what God has said. He will surely fulfill His word. Say from your heart, 'My flesh and my heart faileth; but God is the strength of my heart, and my portion forever.' The victory must be gained day by day."—*Review and Herald*, July 4, 1899.

This passage is based on Luke 11:11-13, where Jesus says: "If a son shall ask bread of any of you that is a father, will he give him a stone? or if he ask a fish, will he for a fish give him a serpent? or if he shall ask an egg, will he offer him a scorpion? If ye then, being evil, know how to give good gifts unto your children: how much more shall your heavenly Father give the Holy Spirit to them that ask him?"

The Holy Spirit enters where needed, and with this presence comes the ability to grant His gifts. Conscious of our innermost wants and emotions, He will without question present one of His special abilities when the right time occurs. We are never to be the judge of this. If we were, we would place ourselves in the shoes of the charismatics who feel they can command God to perform at will.

The Holy Spirit will provide the gift when He deems fit and knowing the circumstances surrounding this need, His actions may be instantaneous. This does not imply that we are not allowed to pray for a gift. We can pray for it; we can desire it; but He will grant the fulfillment of this prayer only when He knows the time has come for godly interference.

The gift of healing, for example, is mentioned as one of the gifts of the Holy Spirit; and being a God of love, He would certainly want His children to have this ability to heal.

When we sense a need—what happens?

There are many instances when friends, relatives, or the elders of a church ask the Holy Spirit to extend the gift of healing to someone who has passed the boundaries of human medical knowledge. When the healing occurs, it is often called the result of a prayer for the sick. In comparison, the apostles' relationship to Christ was so close that their mere order to "rise up and walk" was sufficient exercise in prayer to make the man actually stand up from his sickbed and walk away— healed. These two examples are different yet they contain similarities. They are both manifestations of the gift of healing, but only through the action of the Holy Spirit are they brought into being.

When the healing power of the Holy Spirit reaches out and salvages an individual's human life, it is a miracle; there is no disputing that. But miracles—and it is imperative to keep this always in mind—should only be performed for the edification of the church, the body of Christ, not for the edification of the individual. All of Christ's work can be found within the range of this objective. When Jesus "had compassion" on the afflicted and healed them, He invoked miraculous power to lead all the people's attention to God's power. There was never any effort on Christ's part to win the public's favor because of His miracles. The miracles were used to arrest attention so that He could teach the people or give them a blessing. It was always done with the edification of God in the forefront, and the apostles followed this example. With healing miracles, they worked their way through the New Testament. They preached the word, and miracles happened.

Does Christ or one of His apostles tell us to get up and loudly proclaim and advertise "healing meetings"? Does He encourage us to shout, "I'm gonna heal ya tonight"? No! It was never a goal—always a help—to spread the gospel. That was God's intention.

At present there is much emphasis on claiming the gifts of the Holy Spirit—and not just any gift, but specifically the spectacular ones. The gifts of prophecy, miracles, healing, and tongues have been singled out by thousands the world over to prove that God is with them and that by granting them these gifts, He approves of their way of life.

Not only can this not be Biblically substantiated, but as we have previously emphasized in an earlier chapter, the modern counterfeit manifestations that are to equate these godly gifts indicate a satanic origin and as such have no connection with the gifts of God.

But erring seekers and sincere Christians alike still want the assurance that God will give everyone at least one of His gifts of the Spirit. However, they wonder, What if my gift is not spectacular but one of the more quiet ones such as "teachers" or "governments" (administrative ability)? How can I know for certain that God has singled me out and has really conferred upon me one of the special powers reserved by the Holy Spirit for those who love God?

The secret is that everyone who accepts Christ and is willing to carry out His instructions receives at least one of the gifts of the Spirit. As I look over Paul's list, I see a gift that seems considerably more important than that of governments or tongues; in fact, to me it is the only gift that seems to have been created especially to be a daily manifestation of God-power for use by every Christian—clergyman and laymember alike.

It is the fifth gift on the list.

It is the gift of "helps," as specifically mentioned in 1 Corinthians 12:28. This is a gift I treasure more than any other. It shows me that even though I do not possess the gift to prophesy or to perform miracles or to heal, God has not excluded me when He empowered the Holy Spirit with the ability to distribute the spiritual gifts to His children.

He wants all to be saved; He wants all to leave this troubled world and reign with Him forever; He wants all to have the assurance that the Spirit is impartial; and even though some are especially endowed with gifts that are looked upon as spectacular, the Spirit distributes His gifts to every member of Christ's church. This is another instance where the fruit of the Spirit and the gifts of the Spirit differ. The fruit is a natural consequence; the gifts are special donations that complement the fruitful life—and the one gift we all have is the gift of "helps."

In the entire story surrounding the magnificence of the outpouring of the Holy Spirit, the idea that this all-powerful Being gives every believer the same basic gift, is something that should make every Christian proud. For no true Christian is ever—or has ever been or ever will be—without the ability to be a help to others. This is the only gift that is not confined to making an actual personal contact with another fellow human being. All of the other gifts necessitate a personal encounter in order to make the gift effective, but the gift of "helps" is a quiet and unobtrusive one which everyone regardless of time or circumstance can use.

Perhaps someone feels that he is playing a useless role in the spreading of the gospel because he's restricted to a wheelchair or a sickbed or is totally paralyzed. Don't worry! God has given each the gift of "helps." By encouragement and prayer for others all can perform a service for Christ that is even superior to that of being able to speak another supernaturally supplied foreign language. It is help that humanity needs. It is a gift of such overriding importance that it almost seems all the other spiritual gifts circle around it. For what else does an apostle do but help spread the gospel. And the prophet? Doesn't he convey God's Word to others? And teachers—are they not fulfilling God's desire to help others? What about miracles, and healing? Everyone of the gifts mentioned before that of "helps" in reality is a gift of "helps," but in the instance where it is listed separately, God wants us to use our own Christian initiative and develop this gift, so that it fits in with the different facets of our personality. The others are specific gifts; this one is all-encompassing.

To be a "help" to others covers such a vast range of activities that there may be occasions where the Holy Spirit would want to expand this gift and provide the "helper" with a second or perhaps a third gift of the Spirit, enabling him to carry out his work. Even as the members of a body have to work together in order to create harmonious action, so the various gifts of the spirit must also complement each other—with different gifts going to different members of the church, reaching the various personalities with abilities best suited to their natural makeup.

"There are no two leaves of a tree precisely alike; neither do all minds run in the same direction," writes Ellen White. "But while this is so, there may be unity in diversity. Christ is our root, and all who are grafted into this root will bear the fruit which Christ bore. They will reveal the fragrance of His character in the talent of speech, in the cultivation of hospitality, of kindness, of Christian courtesy and heavenly politeness. Look at the flowers in a carpet, and notice the different colored threads. All are not pink, all are not green, all are not blue. A variety of colors are woven together to perfect the pattern. So it is in the design of God. He has a purpose in placing us where we must learn to live as individuals. We are not all fitted to do the same kind of work, but each man's work is designed by God to make up His plan."—*Review and Herald*, July 4, 1899.

Do you know what is the most beautiful discovery of all? Check the New Testament carefully and you will find that the one who practiced the Spirit's gift of "helps" most of all was Jesus Christ Himself! Everything He preached He practiced by helping humanity attain a higher level of spiritual understanding.

He was God, and He prophesied; He spoke for Himself and the other members of the Trinity on an authoritative level, expressing His will and desires to those He came to rescue. He taught, and in doing so explained His principles, His godly way of life, to people who had lost all understanding of true godliness. When it came to using the gifts of the Spirit—and no one will deny that Christ was filled with the Holy Spirit—the miraculous gifts were used by Christ in the pursuit of creating understanding. He healed in order to glorify God and to draw attention to the power of the Holy Spirit. If it had not been for the awesome power of Christ's medical ministry, many Palestinians might never have heard of Him; yet His healing brought them into close contact with Him, and in many cases, led them directly to an understanding of His mission.

But above everything—He helped. Smiling, compassionately, He stretched out the helping hand of God to all those He met. He recognized the gift of "helps" as a primary way of extending God's hand to everyone in need. The gift of governments He left for those administrators who, in later years, would have to run the affairs of His earthly church. And the gift of tongues? That, too, could wait. His personal love was sufficient when He walked the earth. He practiced love in unlimited magnitude, and His loving help spread from town to town.

Don't ever underestimate the importance or the universal scope of the power of the gift of "helps." Everything Christ did was a magnification of this gift. There remains one important and vital question. Would you rather have a gift that Christ didn't even practice or the one that He used?

Only you can supply the answer.

Only you can make the choice.

other Pacific Press Publishing Association books